Workshop on Active Learning for Natural Language Processing 2010

Held at NAACL HLT 2010

Los Angeles, California, USA
6 June 2010

ISBN: 978-1-61738-670-1

Printed from e-media with permission by:

Curran Associates, Inc.
57 Morehouse Lane
Red Hook, NY 12571

Some format issues inherent in the e-media version may also appear in this print version.

Printed by Curran Associates, Inc. (2010)

Association for Computational Linguistics
209 N. Eighth Street
Stroudsburg, Pennsylvania 18360

Phone: 1-570-476-8006
Fax: 1-570-476-0860

acl@aclweb.org

Additional copies of this publication are available from:

Curran Associates, Inc.
57 Morehouse Lane
Red Hook, NY 12571 USA
Phone: 845-758-0400
Fax: 845-758-2634
Email: curran@proceedings.com
Web: www.proceedings.com

Introduction

Labeled training data is often required to achieve state-of-the-art performance in machine learning solutions to natural language tasks. While traditional supervised learning relies on existing labeled data, *active learning* algorithms may select unlabeled data for labeling with the goal of reducing annotation costs, while maintaining high accuracy. Thus, active learning has emerged as a promising framework for NLP applications and annotation projects where unlabeled data is readily available (e.g., web pages, audio recordings, minority language data), but obtaining labels is cost-prohibitive.

The 2010 Workshop on Active Learning for Natural Language Processing (ALNLP) is the sequel to a successful 2009 meeting of the same name—both co-located with the Annual Conference of the North American Chapter of the Association for Computational Linguistics—with the intent of exploring key practical and theoretical aspects of active learning applied to real-world NLP problems. As we assembled the program committee, the topic's timeliness resonated with researchers both in machine learning (who see natural language as an important application domain for active learning), and with those in language technologies (who see maturing active learning methods as an important part of their toolbox). We feel that the topic is one worth exploring in a focused workshop such as this, at the intersection of these research areas, rather than in occasional isolated papers in various international conference venues. Our aim is to foster innovation and discussion that advances our understanding of active learning for NLP.

Our invited speaker, Jaime Carbonell, has a long history of applying active learning to machine translation, rare class discovery, ranking, and realistic labeling scenarios with multiple imperfect annotators. Given the proliferation of machine learning in language applications, and the growing popularity of online "crowd-sourcing" annotation environments, we expect that these topics with play an important role in the future of active learning for NLP. We are grateful to Dr. Carbonell for agreeing to speak about his new work in these areas.

The workshop received ten submissions, five of which were accepted as oral presentations and are included in the final program. These papers represent the fruit of international researchers exploring a variety of challenges and opportunities in active learning for NLP tasks. These include issues pertinent to human-computer interaction, domain adaptation, and remaining robust to rare class labels and other application-specific issues. We hope that this gathering and these proceedings shed more light on active learning for NLP tasks and the real annotation projects that are required to support them.

We are especially grateful to the program committee, whose reviews were thoughtful and constructive. We also thank all of the researchers who submitted their work for consideration. More information about the workshop is archived online at http://active-learning.net/alnlp2010.

Burr Settles, Kevin Small, and Katrin Tomanek
Workshop Organizers

Organizers:

Burr Settles, Carnegie Mellon University (USA)
Kevin Small, Tufts University (USA)
Katrin Tomanek, University of Jena (Germany)

Program Committee:

Markus Becker, SPSS (an IBM company) (UK)
Claire Cardie, Cornell University (USA)
Hal Daume III, University of Utah (USA)
Ben Hachey, Macquarie University (Australia)
Robbie Haertel, Brigham Young University (USA)
Udo Hahn, University of Jena (Germany)
Eric Horvitz, Microsoft Research (USA)
Rebecca Hwa, University of Pittsburgh (USA)
Ashish Kapoor, Microsoft Research (USA)
Prem Melville, IBM T.J. Watson Research Center (USA)
Ray Mooney, University of Texas at Austin (USA)
Fredrik Olsson, SICS (Sweden)
Foster Provost, New York University (USA)
Eric Ringger, Brigham Young University (USA)
Dan Roth, University of Illinois at Urbana-Champaign (USA)
Burr Settles, Carnegie Mellon University (USA)
Kevin Small, Tufts University (USA)
Katrin Tomanek, University of Jena (Germany)

Additional Reviewers:

Piyush Rai, University of Utah (USA)
Avishek Saha, University of Utah (USA)
Byron Wallace, Tufts University (USA)

Invited Speaker:

Jaime Carbonell, Carnegie Mellon University (USA)

Table of Contents

Workshop Program

Sunday, June 6, 2010

1:00-1:15 Introduction by Burr Settles and Kevin Small

Invited Talk

1:15-2:10 *Active and Proactive Machine Learning: From Fundamentals to Applications in Language Technologies and Beyond* by Jaime Carbonell

Research Papers I

2:10–2:35 *Using Variance as a Stopping Criterion for Active Learning of Frame Assignment*
Masood Ghayoomi

2:35–3:00 *Active Semi-Supervised Learning for Improving Word Alignment*
Vamshi Ambati, Stephan Vogel and Jaime Carbonell

3:00-3:30 **Break**

Research Papers II

3:30–3:55 *D-Confidence: An Active Learning Strategy which Efficiently Identifies Small Classes*
Nuno Escudeiro and Alipio Jorge

3:55–4:20 *Domain Adaptation meets Active Learning*
Piyush Rai, Avishek Saha, Hal Daume and Suresh Venkatasubramanian

4:20–4:55 *Parallel Active Learning: Eliminating Wait Time with Minimal Staleness*
Robbie Haertel, Paul Felt, Eric K. Ringger and Kevin Seppi

4:55-5:30 **Discussion**

Using Variance as a Stopping Criterion for Active Learning of Frame Assignment

Masood Ghayoomi
German Grammar Group
Freie Universität Berlin
Berlin, 14195
masood.ghayoomi@fu-berlin.de

Abstract

Active learning is a promising method to reduce human's effort for data annotation in different NLP applications. Since it is an iterative task, it should be stopped at some point which is optimum or near-optimum. In this paper we propose a novel stopping criterion for active learning of frame assignment based on the variability of the classifier's confidence score on the unlabeled data. The important advantage of this criterion is that we rely only on the unlabeled data to stop the data annotation process; as a result there are no requirements for the gold standard data and testing the classifier's performance in each iteration. Our experiments show that the proposed method achieves 93.67% of the classifier maximum performance.

1 Introduction

Using supervised machine learning methods is very popular in Natural Language Processing (NLP). However, these methods are not applicable for most of the NLP tasks due to the lack of labeled data. Although a huge amount of unlabeled data is freely available, labeling them for supervised learning techniques is very tedious, expensive, time consuming, and error prone.

Active learning is a supervised machine learning method in which informative instances are chosen by the classifier for labeling. Unlike the normal supervised set-up where data annotation and learning are completely independent, active learning is a sequential process (Settles, 2009; Busser and Morante, 2005). This learning method is used in a variety of NLP tasks such as information extraction (Thompson et al., 1999), semantic role labeling (Busser and Morante, 2005), machine translation (Haffari and Sarkar, 2009), and name entity recognition (Laws and Schütze, 2008). In our study, we apply this method for the frame assignment task as a kind of semantic analysis.

The process of active learning is as follows: the learner takes a set of labeled instances, called *seed* data, as an input for initial training of the classifier; and then a larger set of unlabeled instances will be selected by the classifier to be labeled with the human interaction. Even a small set of well selected samples for labeling can achieve the same level of performance of a large labeled data set; and the oracle's effort will be reduced as a result.

The motivation behind active learning is selecting the most useful examples for the classifier and thereby minimizing the annotation effort while still keeping up the performance level (Thompson et al., 1999). There are two major learning scenarios in active learning which are very popular among researchers and frequently used in various NLP tasks: *stream-based sampling* (Cohn et al., 1994) and *pool-based sampling* (Lewis and Gale, 1994).

The samples that are selected should be hard and very informative. There are different query methods for sample selection which are independent of the active learning scenarios (Settles, 2009). Among them, *uncertainty sampling* (Lewis and Gale, 1994) is the most well-known and the simplest sample selection method which only needs one classifier (Baldridge and Osborne, 2004). In this query method, the samples that the classifier is least con-

Proceedings of the NAACL HLT 2010 Workshop on Active Learning for Natural Language Processing, pages 1–9,
Los Angeles, California, June 2010.

Algorithm 1 Uncertainty Sampling in Active Learning

Input: Seed data *S*, Pool of unlabeled samples *U*
Use *S* to train the classifier *C*
while the stopping criterion is met **do**
  Use *C* to annotate *U*
  Select the top *K* samples from *U* predicted by *C* which have the lowest confidence
  Label *K*, augment *S* with the*K* samples, and remove *K* from *U*
  Use *S* to retrain *C*
end while

fident on their labels are selected and handed out to the oracle. To this aim, a confidence score is required which is in fact the prediction of the classifier with the highest probability for the label of the sample (Busser and Morante, 2005).

The approach taken in active learning for our task is based on the uncertainty of the classifier with access to the pool of data. The learning process is presented in Algorithm 1. Since active learning is an iterative process (Busser and Morante, 2005), it should be stopped at some point which is optimum or at least near-optimum. A learning curve is used as a means to illustrate the learning progress of the learner, so that we can monitor the performance of the classifier. In fact, the curve signals when the learning process should stop as almost no increase or even a drop in the performance of the classifier is observed. At this point, additional training data will not increase the performance any more. In this paper, we propose a new stopping criterion based on the variability of the classifier's confidence score on the selected unlabeled data so that we avoid using the labeled gold standard.

The structure of the paper is as follows. In Section 2, we briefly describe *frame semantics* as it is the domain of application for our model. Section 3 introduces our stopping criterion and describes the idea behind it. In Section 4, we describe our data set and present the experimental results. In Section 5, related work on stopping criteria is outlined; and finally Section 6 summarizes the paper.

2 Frame Semantics

Syntactic analysis such as part-of-speech (POS) tagging and parsing has been widely studied and has achieved a great progress. However, semantic analysis did not have such a rapid progress. This problem has recently motivated researches to pay special attention to natural language understanding since it is one of the essential parts in information extraction and question-answering.

Frame semantic structure analysis which is based on the case grammar of Fillmore (1968) is one of the understanding techniques to provide the knowledge about the actions, the participants of the action, and the relations between them. In Fillmore's view, a frame is considered as an abstract scene having some participants as the arguments of the predicate, and some sentences to describe the scene. In fact the frames are the conceptual structures for the background knowledge of the abstract scenes represented by the lexical units and provide context to the elements of the action. FrameNet (Baker and Lowe, 1998) is a data set developed at ICSI Berkley University based on the frame semantics.

In frame semantic structure analysis, the semantic roles of the elements participating in the action are identified. Determining and assigning the semantic roles automatically require two steps: *frame assignment*, and *role assignment* (Erk and Pado, 2006). The first step consists in identifying the frame which is evoked by the predicate to determine the unique frame that is appropriate for the sample. The next step is identifying the arguments of the predicate and assigning the semantic roles to the syntactic arguments of the given frame. In our research, we study the first step, and leave the second step for future work.

3 The Proposed Stopping Criterion

The main idea behind the stopping criteria is to stop the classifier when it has reached its maximum performance and labeling of further examples from the unlabeled data set will not increase the classifier's performance any more. Determining this point is very difficult experimentally without access to the gold standard labels to evaluate the performance; however, we should find a criterion to stop active learning in a near-optimum point. To this aim, we propose a novel stopping criterion which uses the *variance* of the classifier's confidence score for the predicted labels to represent the degree of spreading out the confidence scores around their mean. We hypothesize that there is a correlation between the performance saturation of the classifier and the variability on the confidence of the selected instances.

Generally, as we will see in Section 5, a stopping criterion could be based either on the performance of the classifier on the test data, or on the confidence score of the classifier on the unlabeled data. In our method, we used the second approach. The biggest advantage of this model is that no gold standard data is required to evaluate the performance of the system in each iteration.

3.1 Mean and Variance

Mean and variance are two of the well-known statistical metrics. Mean is a statistical measurement for determining the central tendency among a set of scores. In our study, we have computed the mean (*M*) of the classifier's confidence score for the predicted labels of 5 samples selected in each iteration. Variance is the amount of variability of the scores around their mean. To compute the variability of the classifier's confidence score for the selected samples in each iteration, the following equation is used in our task:

$$Variance = \frac{\sum_{i=1}^{K}(C_i - M)^2}{K} \quad (1)$$

where C_i is the confidence score of each selected sample in each iteration, *M* is the mean of the confidence scores for the predicted labels, and *K* is the number of samples selected in the same iteration (*K*=5 in our study).

3.2 The General Idea

According to the pool-based scenario, in each iteration *K* samples of the extra unlabeled data which have the lowest confidence score are selected, and after labeling by the oracle they are added to the training data. In the early iterations, the mean of the classifier's confidence score for the selected samples is low. Since the classifier is not trained enough in these iterations, most of the scores are low and they do not have a high degree of variability. As a result the variance of the confidence score for these samples is low. We call this step the *untrained* stage of the classifier.

As the classifier is training with more data, the confidence score of the samples will gradually increase; as a result, there will be a high degree of variability in the confidence scores which spread out around their mean. In these iterations, the classifier is relatively in the borderline of the training stage, passing from untrained to trained; so that there will be a high variability of confidence scores which leads to have a high variance. This is the *training* stage of the classifier.

When the classifier is trained, the confidence score of the classifier on the selected samples will increase. However, from a certain point that the classifier is trained enough, all of the confidence scores are located tightly around their mean with a low degree of variability; as a result, the variance of the samples decreases. This is the stage that the classifier is *trained.*

The curve in Figure 1 represents the behavior of the variance in different iterations such that the *x* axis is the number of iterations, and the *y* axis is the variance of the confidence scores in each iteration.

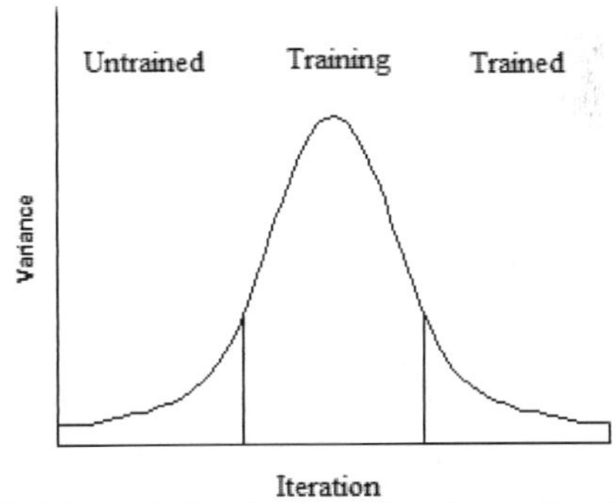

Figure 1: Normal distribution of variance for the classifier's confidence score

Based on our assumption, the best stopping point is when variance reaches its global peak and starts to decrease. In this case, the classifier passes the training stage and enters into the trained stage.

3.3 The Variance Model

It is difficult to determine the peak of the variance on the fly, i.e. without going through all iterations. One easy solution is to stop the learning process as soon as there is a decrease in the variance. However, as it is very likely to stick in the local maxima of the variance curve, this criterion does not work well. In other words, it is possible to have small peaks before reaching the global peak, the highest variability of the classifier's confidence score; so that we might stop at some point we are not interested in and it should be ignored.

To avoid this problem, we propose a model, called *variance model* (VM), to stop active learning when variance (V) decreases in n sequential iterations; i.e.

$$V_i < V_{i-1} < ... < V_{i-n}.$$

There is a possibility that this condition is not satisfied at all in different iterations. In such cases, active learning will not stop and all data will be labeled. This condition is usually met when there are instances in the data which are inherently ambiguous. Having such data is generally unavoidable and it is often problematic for the learner.

Although the above model can deal with the local maxima problem, there is a possibility that the decreased variance in n sequential iterations is very small and it is still possible to stick in the local maxima. To avoid this problem and have a better stopping point, we extend the proposed model by setting a threshold m, called the *Extended Variance Model* (EVM), in which the minimum variance decrement in n sequential iterations must be m; i.e.

$$V_i < V_{i-1} - m < ... < V_{i-n} - m.$$

4 Experimental Results

4.1 Setup of Experiment

What we aim to do in our study is assigning frames with active learning. We have chosen the pool-based scenario by using the uncertainty sampling method. In our task, since we have a small data set, 5 instances (*K*=5) with the lowest confidence score of the predited labels will be selected in each iteration from the pool of data and handed out to the oracle to be labeled.

We have used a toolkit for the supervised word sense disambiguation task called *Majo* (Rehbein et al., 2009) which has a graphical user interface (GUI) for semantic annotation based on active learning. The toolkit supports German and English; and it uses the openNLP MAXENT package[1] to build the model. In this toolkit, the confidence score of the classifier is the posterior probability of the most probable label assigned to each sample.

In addition, there are some built-in plugins in the tool for syntactic and semantic pre-processing to provide the relevant features for the classifier. We utilized the following plugins that support English:

[1]http://maxent.sourceforge.net/

- *Stanford Word Range Plugin* provides features based on the local context of the surface string for the target. The window size of the local context can be set manually in the GUI. Based on initial experiments for the target verbs, we found out that a window ± 3 performs the best.
- *Stanford POS Tag Word Range Plugin* provides the POS tags of the words within a sentence by using Stanford POS Tagger. In this plugin, the window size could also be set manually to extract the POS local context of the target word. Based on initial experiments, a window of ± 3 achieved the best performance.
- *Berkley Sentence Phrase Plugin* utilizes the Berkley Parser and provides the syntactic analysis of the sentence. This plugin is used to extract all word forms of the children nodes from a particular syntactic mother node (VP in our study) and add them to the feature set.
- *Berkley Sentence Phrase POS Tag Plugin* uses the Berkley POS tagger such that we define the mother node of the target word in the parse tree (VP in our study) and it identifies and extracts all children of this mother node and uses their POS as features.

4.2 Corpus

The annotated data that we used for our experiments is the current version of the Berkeley FrameNet (Baker and Lowe, 1998) for English which consists of 139,437 annotated examples from the British National Corpus for 10,196 predicates. Among the predicates that FrameNet involvs, namely verbs, nouns, adjectives, and prepositions, we only considered *verbs*; as a result the data reduced to 61,792 annotated examples for 2,770 unique verb-frames.

In the next step, we removed all verbs that have only one frame as they are not ambiguous. Having only ambiguous verbs, the number of predicates reduced to 451 unique verbs. Out of these targets, there are only 37 verbs which have more than 100 annotated samples. Among these verbs, we concentrated on 14 verbs selected randomly; however, in the selection we tried to have a balance distribution of frames that the targets have. Therefore, we selected 4 targets (*phone*, *rush*, *scream*, *throw*) with

Table 1: Data distribution of the targets

Verb	Frames	Freq.	S	E	T
Bend	4	115	11	82	22
Feel	5	134	13	95	26
Follow	3	113	10	81	22
Forget	3	101	9	72	20
Hit	4	142	12	102	28
Look	3	183	15	134	34
Phone	2	166	14	121	31
Rise	4	110	11	77	22
Rush	2	168	14	123	31
Scream	2	148	12	108	28
Shake	4	104	10	73	21
Smell	3	146	13	106	27
Strike	3	105	10	75	20
Throw	2	155	13	113	29

two frames, 5 targets (*follow*, *forget*, *look*, *smell*, *strike*) with three frames, 4 targets (*bend*, *hit*, *rise*, *shake*) with four frames, and 1 target (*feel*) with five frames.

4.3 Data Distribution

The total amount of data prepared for the 14 verbs are divided into three non-overlapping sets in a balanced form in terms of both the number of the target predicate frames, and the relevant instances of each frame. In other words, the distribution should be such that different frames of the target verb is found in each of the three data sets. 10% is considered as initial seed data (S); 20% as test data (T), and the rest of 70% as extra unlabeled data (E). Table 1 presents the data distribution in which 5-fold cross-validation is performed to minimize the overfitting problem.

As mentioned, our proposed stopping criterion has two parameters, n and m, that should be tuned. For this purpose, we divided the 14 targets into the held-out set and the test set. To this aim, 7 targets, namely *feel*, *look*, *phone*, *rise*, *shake*, *smell*, and *throw* are selected as the held-out set; and 7 targets, namely *bend*, *follow*, *forget*, *hit*, *rush*, *scream*, and *strike* are used as the test set.

4.4 Results

Figures 2 and 3 illustrate the learning curves of the active learning process and random sampling as the baseline for the targets *look* and *rise*. The curves are the average of the 5 folds. As can be seen, in these targets our classifier has beaten the majority

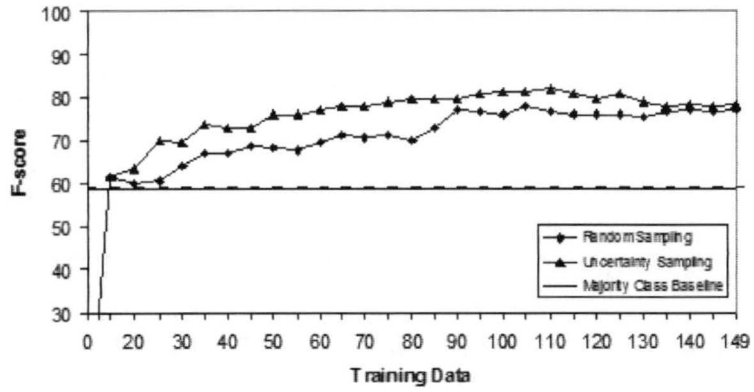

Figure 2: Learning curve of the verb *look* for 5 folds

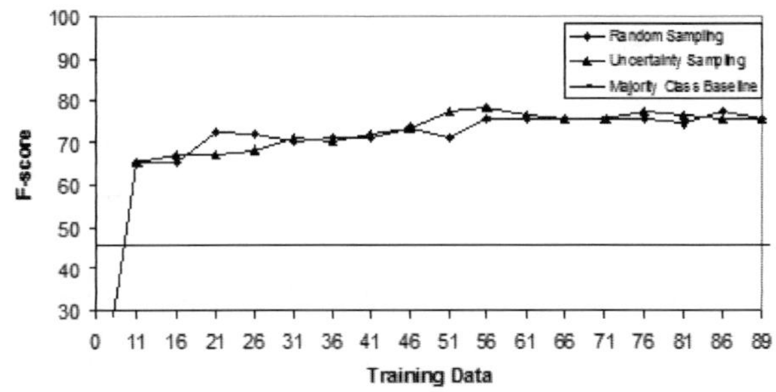

Figure 3: Learning curve of the verb *rise* for 5 folds

class baseline; and also active learning with uncertainty sampling has a relatively better performance than random sampling.

Figures 4 and 5 present the average variance curves of 5 folds for the two targets. These curves verify our assumption about the behavior of the variance curve as described in Section 3.2. As the graphs show, following our assumption the variability around the mean is tight in the early stages of training; then as the classifier is trained with more data, the variability around the mean spreads out; and finally, the variability will be tight again around the mean.

Applying our proposed stopping criterion, in each iteration we compute the variance of the classifier's confidence score for the selected samples in each fold. To evaluate how well our stopping criterion is, we have compared our results with the maximum average performance of the classifier for the 5 folds in which the whole data is labeled.

Applying our model on the held-out set, we found that n=2 is the best value based on our data set, so that we stop active learning when variance decreases in two sequential iterations; i.e.

$$V_i < V_{i-1} \text{ and } V_{i-1} < V_{i-2}.$$

Our idea is shown in Figure 6 for fold 5 of the target *rise*, such that the proposed stopping criterion is satisfied in iteration 11. As shown, the decrement of

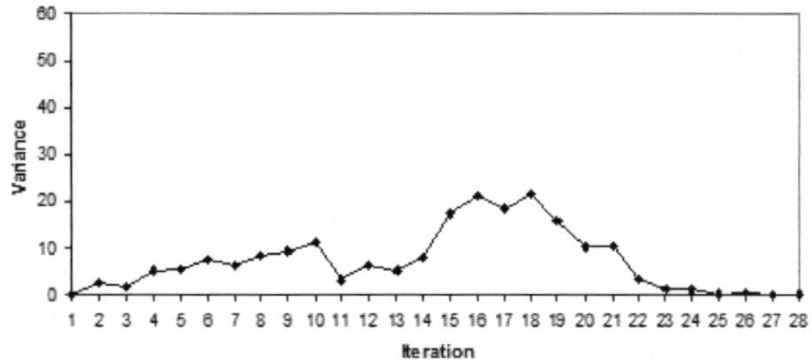

Figure 4: Variance curve of the verb *look* for 5 folds

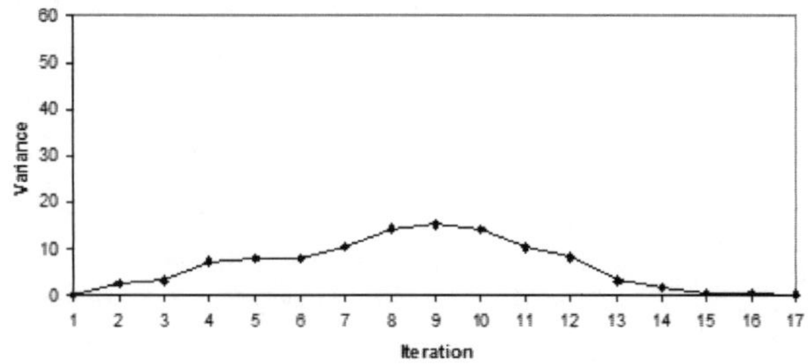

Figure 5: Variance curve of the verb *rise* for 5 folds

variance in iterations 3, 5, and 7 is the local maxima so that active learning does not stop in these iterations and they are ignored.

The summary of the result for the uncertainty sampling method of the test set is shown in Table 2 in which the F-score serves as the evaluation metric. Comparing the applied variance model as the stopping criterion on the test set with the maximum performance (M) of the uncertainty sampling as an upper bound in our experiment, we see that for two targets (*bend*, *rush*) the maximum performance of the classifier is achieved at the stopping point; for two targets (*follow*, *hit*) there is a minor reduction in the performance; while for the other targets (*forget*, *scream*, *strike*) there is a big loss in the performance. Averagely, the variance model achieved 92.66% of the maximum performance.

To determine the advantage of our stopping criterion, we present the total numbers of annotated instances (A) for each target, their relevant numbers of annotated instances for the maximum performance, and the variance model in Table 3. Av-

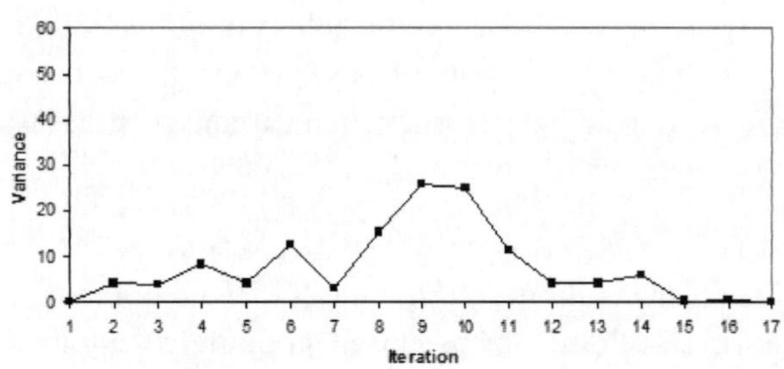

Figure 6: Variance curve of the verb *rise*

Table 2: The comparison of the average performance of the classifier (F-score) on the stopping point with the maximum performance in uncertainty sampling

Verb	M	VM
Bend	53.00	53.00
Follow	71.81	70.00
Forget	51.00	41.00
Hit	65.71	63.56
Rush	89.03	89.03
Scream	72.14	62.85
Strike	64.00	53.00
Average	**66.67**	**61.78**

Table 3: The comparison of the number of the annotated data for all data, at the maximum performance, and at the stopping point

Verb	A	M	VM
Bend	93	46	55
Follow	91	75	54
Forget	81	79	51
Hit	114	67	71
Rush	137	24	51
Scream	120	62	64
Strike	85	85	41
Average	**103**	**62.57**	**55.29**

eragely, if we have 103 samples for annotation, we need to annotate almost 63 instances to reach the maximum performance of 66.67%; while by applying our stopping criterion, the learning process stops by annotating at least 55 instances with 61.78% performance. I.e., annotating a smaller number of instances, our active learner achieves a near-optimum performance. It is worth to mention that since it is very difficult to achieve the upper bound of the classifier's performance automatically, all data is labeled to find the maximum performance of the classifier.

Looking carefully on the variance curves of the 5 folds of the held-out set, we have seen that in some iterations the decreased variance in two sequential iterations is very small and it may still stick in the local maxima as can be seen in iteration 8 of fold 3 of the target *look* in Figure 7.

To avoid sticking in such local maxima, we used the extended version of our original model and set a threshold (m) in the held-out set. Experimentally we found out that the decreasing variance in two sequential iterations must be bigger than 0.5; i.e.

$$V_i < V_{i-1} - 0.5 \text{ and } V_{i-1} < V_{i-2} - 0.5;$$

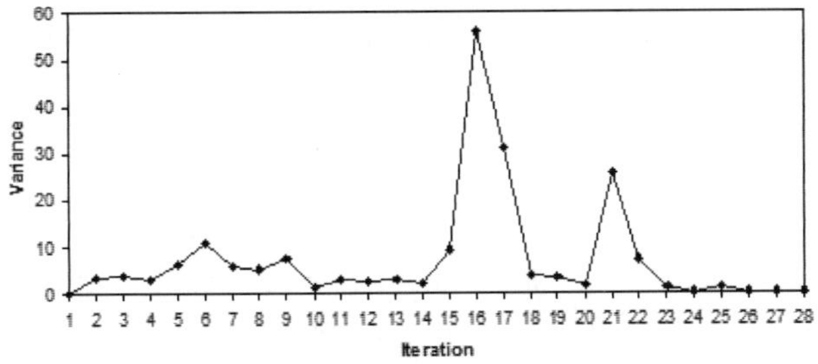

Figure 7: Variance curve of the verb *look*

so that in Figure 7 we stop in iteration 18. We applied the extended variance model on the test set and compared the results to our original variance model. We found out for two targets (*forget*, *scream*) the extended model has achieved a very good performance; for four targets (*follow*, *hit*, *rush*, *strike*) it was ineffective; and for one target (*bend*) it caused to have a small reduction in the performance.

The summary of the classifier performance after applying the extended model for uncertainty sampling is shown in Table 4. To ease the comparison, the performance of our original model is repeated in this table. As presented in the table, the average performance in the extended model has a 13.70% relative improvement compared to the average performance in the original variance model.

Table 4: The comparison of the average performance of the classifier (F-score) on the variance model and the extended variance model

Verb	VM	EM
Bend	53.00	52.00
Follow	70.00	70.00
Forget	41.00	46.00
Hit	63.56	63.56
Rush	89.03	89.03
Scream	62.85	63.56
Strike	53.00	53.00
Average	**61.78**	**62.45**

5 Related Work on Stopping Criteria

The simplest stopping criterion for active learning is when the training set has reached a desirable size or a predefined threshold. In this criterion, the active learning process repeatedly provides informative examples to the oracle for labeling, and updates the training set, until the desired size is obtained or the predefined stopping criterion is met. Practically, it is not clear how much annotation is sufficient for inducing a classifier with maximum effectiveness (Lewis and Gale, 1994).

Schohn and Cohn (2000) have used support vector machines (SVM) for document classification using the selective sampling method and they have proposed a criterion to stop the learning process in their task. Based on their idea, when there is no informative instance in the pool which is closer to the separating hyperplane than any of the support vectors, the margin exhausts and the learning process stops.

Zhu and Hovey (2007) have used a confidence-based approach for the stopping criteria by utlizing the *maximum confidence* and the *minimum error* of the classifier. The maximum confidence is based on the uncertainty measurement when the entropy of the selected unlabeled sample is less than a predefined threshold close to zero. The minimum error is the feedback from the oracle when active learning asks for the true label of the selected unlabeled sample and the accuracy prediction of the classifier for the selected unlabeled sample is larger than a predefined accuracy threshold. These criteria are considered as upper-bound and lower-bound of the stopping condition.

Zhu et al. (2008) proposed another stopping criterion based on a statistical learning approach called *minimum expected error strategy*. In this approach, the maximum effectiveness of the classifier is reached when the classifier's expected errors on future unlabeled data is minimum.

Vlachos (2008) has used the classifier confidence score as a stopping criterion for the uncertainty sampling. He has applied his model to two NLP tasks: text classification and named entity recognition. He has built his models with the SVM and the maximum entropy. The idea is when the confidence of the classifier remains at the same level or drops for a number of consecutive iterations, the learning process should terminate.

Laws and Schütze (2008) suggested three criteria -*minimal absolute performance*, *maximum possible performance*, and *convergence*- to stop active learning for name entity recognition using the SVM model with the uncertainty sampling method. In minimal absolute performance, a threshold is predefined by the user; and then the classifier estimates its own performance by using only the unlabeled reference test set. Since there is no available labeled test set, the evaluation performance is not possible. The maximum possible performance is a confidence-based stopping criterion in which active learning is stopped where the optimal performance of the classifier is achieved. Again, in this approach there is no labeled test data to evaluate the performance. The convergence criterion is met when more examples from the pool of unlabeled data do not contribute more information to the classifier's performance, so that the classifier has reached its maximum performance. Laws and Schütze computed the convergence as the gradient of the classifier's estimated performance or uncertainty.

Tomanek and Hahn (2008) proposed a stopping criterion based on the performance of the classifier without requiring a labeled gold standard for a committee-based active learning on the name entity recognition application. In their criterion, they approximated the progression of the learning curve based on the disagreement among the committee members. They have used the *validation set agreement* curve as an adequate approximation for the progression of the learning curve. This curve was based on the data in each active learning iteration that makes the agreement values comparable between different active learning iterations.

Bloodgood and Vijay-Shanker (2009) explained three areas of stopping active learning that should be improved: applicability (restricting the usage in certain situation), lack of aggressive stopping (finding the stopping points which are too far, so more examples than necessary are annotated), instability (well working of a method on some data set but not the other data set). Further, they presented a stopping criterion based on *stabilizing predictions* that addresses each of the above three areas and provides a user-adjustable stopping behavior. In this method, the prediction of active learning was tested on examples which do not have to be labeled and it is stopped when the predictions are stabilized. This criterion was applied to text classification and named entity recognition tasks using the SVM and the maximum entropy models.

6 Summary and Future Work

In this paper, after a brief overview of frame semantics and active learning scenarios and query methods, we performed the frame assignment in the pool-based active learning with the uncertainty sampling method. To this end, we chose 14 frequent targets from FrameNet data set for our task.

One of the properties of active learning is its iterativness which should be stopped when the classifier has reached its maximum performance. Reaching this point is very difficult; therefore, we proposed a stopping criterion which stops active learning in a near-optimum point. This stopping criterion is based on the confidence score of the classifier on the extra unlabeled data such that it uses the variance of the classifier's confidence score for the predicted labels of a certain number of samples selected in each iteration. The advantage of this criterion is that there is no need to the labeled gold standard data and testing the performance of the classifier in each iteration. Based on this idea, we proposed a model which is satisfied by n sequential decrease on a variance curve. The original model is expanded by setting a threshold m on the amount of the decrement of variance in n sequential iterations. We believe that our proposed criterion can be applied to any active learning setting based on uncertainty sampling and it is not limited to the frame assignment.

To find out how effective our model is, we compared the achieved results of our variance model with the maximum performance of the classifier and we found that 92.66% of the performance is kept in the test data. In the extended variance model, we achieved a higher performance of the classifier in which 93.67% of the performance is kept.

For the future word, while in our current research the learner selects 5 instances in each iteration, this number could be different and investigation is needed to find out how much our proposed criterion depends on the K. The other possibility to expand our proposed model is using the variance of the classifier's confidence score for the predicted labels of the whole unlabeled data in each iteration and not the selected samples.

7 Acknowledgments

The author's special gratitude goes to Caroline Sporleder and Ines Rehbein at Saarland University for their support and helpful comments in the research. Masood Ghayoomi is funded by the German research council DFG under the contract number MU 2822/3-1.

References

C. F. Baker and C. J. Fillmore J. B. Lowe. 1998. The berkeley framenet project. In *Proceedings of ACL*, pages 86–90, Montreal, QC.

J. Baldridge and M. Osborne. 2004. Active learning and the total cost of annotation. In *Proceedings of EMNLP*, pages 9–16, Barcelona, Spain.

M. Bloodgood and K. Vijay-Sarkar. 2009. A method for stopping active learning based on stabilizing predictions and the need for user-adjustable stopping. In *13th Conf. on Computational Natural Language Learning*, pages 39–47, Boulder, Colorado.

B. Busser and R. Morante. 2005. Designing an active learning based system for corpus annotation. In *Revista de Procesamiento del Lenguaje Natural*, number 35, pages 375–381.

D. Cohn, A. L. Atlas, and R. E. Ladner. 1994. Improving generalization with active learning. *Machine Learning*, 15(2):201–221.

K. Erk and S. Pado. 2006. Shalmaneser - a toolchain for shallow semantic parsing. In *Proceedings of LREC*, Genoa, Italy.

C. J. Fillmore. 1968. The case for case. In Emmon W. Bach and Robert T. Harms, editors, *Universals in Linguistic Theory*, pages 1–88, New York. Rinehart and Winston.

G. Haffari and A. Sarkar. 2009. Active learning for multilingual statistical machine translation. In *Proceedings of the 47th ACL-IJCNLP*, Singapore.

F. Laws and H. Schütze. 2008. Stopping criteria for active learning of named entity recognition. In *Proceedings of the 22nd CoLing*, pages 465–472, Manchester.

D.D. Lewis and W. Gale. 1994. A sequential algorithm for training text classifiers. In *Proceedings of the ACM SIGIR Conf. on Research and Development in IR*, pages 3–12.

I. Rehbein, J. Ruppenhofer, and J. Sunde. 2009. Majo - a toolkit for supervised word sense disambiguation and active learning. In *Proceedings of the 8th Int. Workshop on Treebanks and Linguistic Theories*, Milan, Italy.

G. Schohn and D. Cohn. 2000. Less is more: Active learning with support vector machines. In *Proceedings of 17th Int. Conf. on Machine Learning*, Stanford University.

B. Settles. 2009. Active learning literature survey. Computer Sciences Technical Report 1648, University of Wisconsin–Madison.

C. A. Thompson, M.E. Califf, and R.J. Mooney. 1999. Active learning for natural language parsing and information extraction. In *Proceedings of the 16th Int. Conf. on Machine Learning*, pages 406–414.

K. Tomanek and U. Hahn. 2008. Approximating learning curves for active-learning-driven annotation. In *6th Int. Language Resources and Evaluation Conference*, pages 1319–1324.

A. Vlachos. 2008. A stopping criterion for active learning. *Journal of Computer, Speech and Language*, 22(3):295–312.

J. Zhu and E. Hovy. 2007. Active learning for word sense disambiguation with methods for addressing the class imbalance problem. In *Proceedings of the EMNLP-CoNLL*, pages 783–790, Prague.

J. Zhu, H. Wang, and E. Hovy. 2008. Learning a stopping criterion for active learning for word sense disambiguation and text classification. In *Proceedings of the 3rd IJNLP*, pages 366–372, Heydarabad, India.

Active Semi-Supervised Learning for Improving Word Alignment

Vamshi Ambati, Stephan Vogel and Jaime Carbonell
{vamshi,vogel,jgc}@cs.cmu.edu
Language Technologies Institute, Carnegie Mellon University
5000 Forbes Avenue, Pittsburgh, PA 15213, USA

Abstract

Word alignment models form an important part of building statistical machine translation systems. Semi-supervised word alignment aims to improve the accuracy of automatic word alignment by incorporating full or partial alignments acquired from humans. Such dedicated elicitation effort is often expensive and depends on availability of bilingual speakers for the language-pair. In this paper we study active learning query strategies to carefully identify highly uncertain or most informative alignment links that are proposed under an unsupervised word alignment model. Manual correction of such informative links can then be applied to create a labeled dataset used by a semi-supervised word alignment model. Our experiments show that using active learning leads to maximal reduction of alignment error rates with reduced human effort.

1 Introduction

The success of statistical approaches to Machine Translation (MT) can be attributed to the IBM models (Brown et al., 1993) that characterize *word-level* alignments in parallel corpora. Parameters of these alignment models are learnt in an unsupervised manner using the EM algorithm over *sentence-level* aligned parallel corpora. While the ease of automatically aligning sentences at the word-level with tools like GIZA++ (Och and Ney, 2003) has enabled fast development of statistical machine translation (SMT) systems for various language pairs, the quality of alignment is typically quite low for language pairs that diverge from the independence assumptions made by the generative models. Also, an immense amount of parallel data enables better estimation of the model parameters, but a large number of language pairs still lack parallel data.

Two directions of research have been pursued for improving generative word alignment. The first is to relax or update the independence assumptions based on more information, usually syntactic, from the language pairs (Cherry and Lin, 2006). The second is to use extra annotation, typically *word-level* human alignment for some sentence pairs, in conjunction with the parallel data to learn alignment in a semi-supervised manner. Our research is in the direction of the latter, and aims to reduce the effort involved in hand-generation of word alignments by using active learning strategies for careful selection of word pairs to seek alignment.

Active learning for MT has not yet been explored to its full potential. Much of the literature has explored one task – selecting sentences to translate and add to the training corpus (Haffari et al., 2009). In this paper we explore active learning for word alignment, where the input to the active learner is a sentence pair (s_1^J, t_1^I), present in two different languages $\mathcal{S} = \{s^*\}$ and $\mathcal{T} = \{t^*\}$, and the annotation elicited from human is a set of links $\{(j,i) : j = 0 \cdots J; i = 0 \cdots I\}$. Unlike previous approaches, our work does not require elicitation of full alignment for the sentence pair, which could be effort-intensive. We use standard active learning query strategies to selectively elicit partial alignment information. This partial alignment information is then fed into a semi-supervised word aligner which per-

Proceedings of the NAACL HLT 2010 Workshop on Active Learning for Natural Language Processing, pages 10–17,
Los Angeles, California, June 2010.

forms an improved word alignment over the entire parallel corpus.

Rest of the paper is organized as follows. We present related work in Section 2. Section 3 gives an overview of unsupervised word alignment models and its semi-supervised improvisation. Section 4 details our active learning framework with discussion of the link selection strategies in Section 5. Experiments in Section 6 have shown that our selection strategies reduce alignment error rates significantly over baseline. We conclude with discussion on future work.

2 Related Work

Semi-supervised learning is a broader area of Machine Learning, focusing on improving the learning process by usage of unlabeled data in conjunction with labeled data (Chapelle et al., 2006). Many semi-supervised learning algorithms use co-training framework, which assumes that the dataset has multiple views, and training different classifiers on a non-overlapping subset of these features provides additional labeled data (Zhu, 2005). Active query selection for training a semi-supervised learning algorithm is an interesting method that has been applied to clustering problems. Tomanek and Hahn (2009) applied active semi supervised learning to the sequence-labeling problem. Tur et al. (2005) describe active and semi-supervised learning methods for reducing labeling effort for spoken language understanding. They train supervised classification algorithms for the task of call classification and apply it to a large unlabeled dataset to select the least confident instances for human labeling.

Researchers have begun to explore semi-supervised word alignment models that use both labeled and unlabeled data. Fraser and Marcu (2006) pose the problem of alignment as a search problem in log-linear space with features coming from the IBM alignment models. The log-linear model is trained on the available labeled data to improve performance. They propose a semi-supervised training algorithm which alternates between discriminative error training on the labeled data to learn the weighting parameters and maximum-likelihood EM training on unlabeled data to estimate the parameters. Callison-Burch et al. (2004) also improve alignment by interpolating human alignments with automatic alignments. They observe that while working with such datasets, alignments of higher quality should be given a much higher weight than the lower-quality alignments. Wu et al. (2006) learn separate models from labeled and unlabeled data using the standard EM algorithm. The two models are then interpolated as a learner in the semi-supervised AdaBoost algorithm to improve word alignment.

Active learning has been applied to various fields of Natural Language Processing like statistical parsing, entity recognition among others (Hwa, 2004; Tang et al., 2001; Shen et al., 2004). In case of MT, the potential of active learning has remained largely unexplored. For Statistical Machine Translation, application of active learning has been focused on the task of selecting the most informative sentences to train the model, in order to reduce cost of data acquisition. Recent work in this area discussed multiple query selection strategies for a Statistical Phrase Based Translation system (Haffari et al., 2009). Their framework requires source text to be translated by the system and the translated data is used in a self-training setting to train MT models. To our knowledge, we are not aware of any work that has looked at reducing human effort by selective elicitation of alignment information using active learning techniques.

3 Word Alignment

3.1 IBM models

IBM models provide a generative framework for performing word alignment of parallel corpus. Given two strings from source and target languages $s_1^J = s_1, \cdots, s_j, \cdots s_J$ and $t_1^I = t_1, \cdots, t_i, \cdots t_I$, an alignment $\mathcal{A}$ is defined as a subset of the Cartesian product of the word indices as shown in Eq 1. In IBM models, since alignment is treated as a function, all the source positions must be covered exactly once (Brown et al., 1993).

$$\mathcal{A} \subseteq \{(j,i) : j = 0 \cdots J; i = 0 \cdots I\} \tag{1}$$

For the task of translation, we would ideally want to model $P(s_1^I|t_1^J)$, which is the probability of observing source sentence s_1^I given target sentence t_1^J. This requires a lot of parallel corpus for estimation and so it is then factored over the word alignment A for the sentence pair, which is a hidden variable. Word alignment is therefore a by-product in the process of modeling translation. We can also represent the same under some parameterization of θ, which is the model we are interested to estimate.

$$P(s_1^J|t_1^I) = \sum_{a_1^J} Pr(s_1^J, A|t_1^J) \quad (2)$$

$$= \sum_{A} p_\theta(s_1^J, A|t_1^I) \quad (3)$$

Given a parallel corpus U of sentence pairs $\{(s_k, t_k) : k = 1, \cdots, K\}$ the parameters can be estimated by maximizing the conditional likelihood over the data. IBM models (Brown et al., 1993) from 1 to 5 are different ways of factoring the probability model to estimate the parameter set θ. For example in the simplest of the models, IBM model 1, only the lexical translation probability is considered treating each word being translated independent of the other words.

$$\hat{\theta} = \arg\max_\theta \prod_{k=1}^{K} \sum_{A} p_\theta(s_k, A|t_k) \quad (4)$$

The parameters of the model above are estimated as $\hat{\theta}$, using the EM algorithm. We can also extract the *Viterbi alignment* ,$\hat{A}$, for all the sentence pairs, which is the alignment with the highest probability under the current model parameters θ:

$$\hat{A} = \arg\max_A p_{\hat{\theta}}(s_1^J, A|t_1^I) \quad (5)$$

The alignment models are asymmetric and differ with the choice of translation direction. We can therefore perform the above after switching the direction of the language pair and obtain models and Viterbi alignments for the corpus as represented below:

$$\hat{\theta} = \arg\max_\theta \prod_{k=1}^{K} \sum_{a} p_\theta(t_k, a|s_k) \quad (6)$$

$$\hat{A} = \arg\max_A p_{\hat{\theta}}(t_1^I, A|s_1^J) \quad (7)$$

Given the Viterbi alignment for each sentence pair in the parallel corpus, we can also compute the word-level alignment probabilities using simple relative likelihood estimation for both the directions. As we will discuss in Section 5, the alignments and the computed lexicons form an important part of our link selection strategies.

$$P(s_j/t_i) = \frac{\sum_s count(t_i, s_j; \hat{A})}{\sum_s count(t_i)} \quad (8)$$

$$P(t_i/s_j) = \frac{\sum_s count(t_i, s_j; \hat{A})}{\sum_s count(s_j)} \quad (9)$$

We perform all our experiments on a symmetrized alignment that combines the bidirectional alignments using heuristics as discussed in (Koehn et al., 2007). We represent this alignment as $A = \{a_{ij} : i = 0 \cdots J \in s_1^J; j = 0 \cdots I \in t_1^I\}$.

3.2 Semi-Supervised Word Alignment

We use an extended version of MGIZA++ (Gao and Vogel, 2008) to perform the constrained semi-supervised word alignment. To get full benefit from the manual alignments, MGIZA++ modifies all alignment models used in the standard training procedure, i.e. the IBM1, HMM, IBM3 and IBM4 models. Manual alignments are incorporated in the EM training phase of these models as constraints that restrict the summation over all possible alignment paths. Typically in the EM procedure for IBM models, the training procedure requires for each source sentence position, the summation over all positions in the target sentence. The manual alignments allow for one-to-many alignments and many-to-many alignments in both directions. For each position i in the source sentence, there can be more than one manually aligned target word. The restricted training will allow only those paths, which are consistent with the manual alignments. Therefore, the restriction of the alignment paths reduces to restricting the summation in EM.

4 Active Learning for Word Alignment

Active learning attempts to optimize performance by selecting the most informative instances to label, where 'informativeness' is defined as maximal expected improvement in accuracy. The objective is to select optimal instance for an external expert to label and then run the learning method on the newly-labeled and previously-labeled instances to minimize prediction or translation error, repeating until either the maximal number of external queries is reached or a desired accuracy level is achieved. Several studies (Tong and Koller, 2002; Nguyen and Smeulders, 2004; Donmez and Carbonell, 2008) show that active learning greatly helps to reduce the labeling effort in various classification tasks.

We discuss our active learning setup for word alignment in Algorithm 1. We start with an unlabeled dataset $U = \{(S_k, T_k)\}$, indexed by k, and a seed pool of partial alignment links $A_0 = \{a_{ij}^k, \forall s_i \in S_k, t_j \in T_k\}$. Each a_{ij}^k represents an alignment link from a sentence pair k that connects source word s_i with t_j.

This is usually an empty set at iteration $t = 0$. We iterate for T iterations. We take a pool-based active learning strategy, where we have access to all the automatically aligned links and we can score the links based on our active learning query strategy. The query strategy uses the automatically trained alignment model θ_t from the current iteration t, for scoring the links. Re-training and re-tuning an SMT system for each link at a time is computationally infeasible. We therefore perform batch learning by selecting a set of N links scored high by our query strategy. We seek manual corrections for the selected links and add the alignment data to the current labeled dataset. The word-level aligned labeled dataset is then provided to our semi-supervised word alignment algorithm, which uses it to produces the alignment model θ_{t+1} for U.

Algorithm 1 AL FOR WORD ALIGNMENT

```
Unlabeled Data Set: U = {(s_k, t_k)}
Manual Alignment Set : A_0 = {a^k_ij, ∀s_i ∈ S_k, t_j ∈ T_k}
Train Semi-supervised Word Alignment using (U, A_0) → θ_0
N: batch size
for t = 0 to T do
    L_t = LinkSelection(U, A_t, θ_t, N)
    Request Human Alignment for L_t
    A_{t+1} = A_t + L_t
    Re-train Semi-Supervised Word Alignment on (U, A_{t+1}) → θ_{t+1}
end for
```

We can iteratively perform the algorithm for a defined number of iterations T or until a certain desired performance is reached, which is measured by alignment error rate (AER) (Fraser and Marcu, 2007) in the case of word alignment. In a more typical scenario, since reducing human effort or cost of elicitation is the objective, we iterate until the available budget is exhausted.

5 Query Strategies for Link Selection

We propose multiple query selection strategies for our active learning setup. The scoring criteria is designed to select alignment links across sentence pairs that are highly uncertain under current automatic translation models. These links are difficult to align correctly by automatic alignment and will cause incorrect phrase pairs to be extracted in the translation model, in turn hurting the translation quality of the SMT system. Manual correction of such links produces the maximal benefit to the model. We would ideally like to elicit the least number of manual corrections possible in order to reduce the cost of data acquisition. In this section we discuss our link selection strategies based on the standard active learning paradigm of 'uncertainty sampling'(Lewis and Catlett, 1994). We use the automatically trained translation model θ_t for scoring each link for uncertainty. In particular θ_t consists of bidirectional lexicon tables computed from the bidirectional alignments as discussed in Section 3.

5.1 Uncertainty based: Bidirectional Alignment Scores

The automatic Viterbi alignment produced by the alignment models is used to obtain translation lexicons, as discussed in Section 3. These lexicons capture the conditional distributions of source-given-target $P(s/t)$ and target-given-source $P(t/s)$ probabilities at the word level where $s_i \in S$ and $t_j \in T$. We define certainty of a link as the harmonic mean of the bidirectional probabilities. The selection strategy selects the least scoring links according to the formula below which corresponds to links with maximum uncertainty:

$$Score(a_{ij}/s_1^I, t_1^J) = \frac{2 * P(t_j/s_i) * P(s_i/t_j)}{P(t_j/s_i) + P(s_i/t_j)} \quad (10)$$

5.2 Confidence Based: Posterior Alignment probabilities

Confidence estimation for MT output is an interesting area with meaningful initial exploration (Blatz et al., 2004; Ueffing and Ney, 2007). Given a sentence pair (s_1^I, t_1^J) and its word alignment, we compute two confidence metrics at alignment link level – based on the posterior link probability and a simple IBM Model 1 as seen in Equation 13. We select the alignment links that the initial word aligner is least confident according to our metric and seek manual correction of the links. We use $t2s$ to denote computation using higher order (IBM4) target-given-source models and $s2t$ to denote source-given-target models. Targeting some of the uncertain parts of word alignment has already been shown to improve translation quality in SMT (Huang, 2009). In our current work, we use confidence metrics as an active learning sampling strategy to obtain most informative links. We also experiment with other confidence metrics as discussed in (Ueffing and Ney, 2007), especially the IBM 1 model score metric which showed some improvement as well.

$$P_{t2s}(a_{ij}, t_1^J/s_1^I) = \frac{p_{t2s}(t_j/s_i, a_{ij} \in A)}{\sum_i^M p_{t2s}(t_j/s_i)} \quad (11)$$

$$P_{s2t}(a_{ij}, s_1^I/t_1^J) = \frac{p_{s2t}(s_i/t_j, a_{ij} \in A)}{\sum_i^N p_{t2s}(t_j/s_i)} \quad (12)$$

$$Conf(a_{ij}/S,T) = \frac{2 * P_{t2s} * P_{s2t}}{P_{t2s} + P_{s2t}} \quad (13)$$

5.3 Agreement Based: Query by Committee

The generative alignments produced differ based on the choice of direction of the language pair. We use A_{s2t} to denote alignment in the source to target direction and A_{t2s} to denote the target to source direction. We consider these alignments to be two experts that have two different views of the alignment process. We formulate our query strategy to select links, where the agreement differs across these two alignments. In general query by committee is a standard sampling strategy in active learning(Freund et al., 1997), where the committee consists of any number of experts with varying opinions, in this case alignments in different directions. We formulate a query by committee sampling strategy for word alignment as shown in Equation 14. In order to break ties, we extend this approach to select the link with higher average frequency of occurrence of words involved in the link.

Language	Sentences	Words	
		Src	Tgt
Ch-En	21,863	424,683	524,882
Ar-En	29,876	630,101	821,938

Table 1: Corpus Statistics of Human Data

Alignment	Automatic Links	Manual Links
Ch-En	491,887	588,075
Ar-En	786,223	712,583

Table 2: Alignment Statistics of Human Data

$$Score(a_{ij}) = \alpha \quad \text{where} \quad (14)$$

$$\alpha = \begin{cases} 2 & a_{ij} \in A_{t2s} \cap A_{t2s} \\ 1 & a_{ij} \in A_{t2s} \cup A_{t2s} \\ 0 & otherwise \end{cases}$$

6 Experiments

6.1 Data Analysis

To run our active learning and semi-supervised word alignment experiments iteratively, we simulate the setup by using a parallel corpus for which the gold standard human alignment is already available. We experiment with two language pairs - Chinese-English and Arabic-English. Corpus-level statistics for both language pairs can be seen in Table 1 and their alignment link level statistics can be seen in Table 2. Both datasets were released by LDC as part of the GALE project.

Chinese-English dataset consists of 21,863 sentence pairs with complete manual alignment. The human alignment for this dataset is much denser than the automatic word alignment. On an average each source word is linked to more than one target word. Similarly, the Arabic-English dataset consisting of 29,876 sentence pairs also has a denser manual alignment. Automatic word alignment in both cases was computed as a symmetrized version of the bidirectional alignments obtained from using GIZA++ (Och and Ney, 2003) in each direction separately.

6.2 Word Alignment Results

We first perform an unsupervised word alignment of the parallel corpus. We then use the learned model

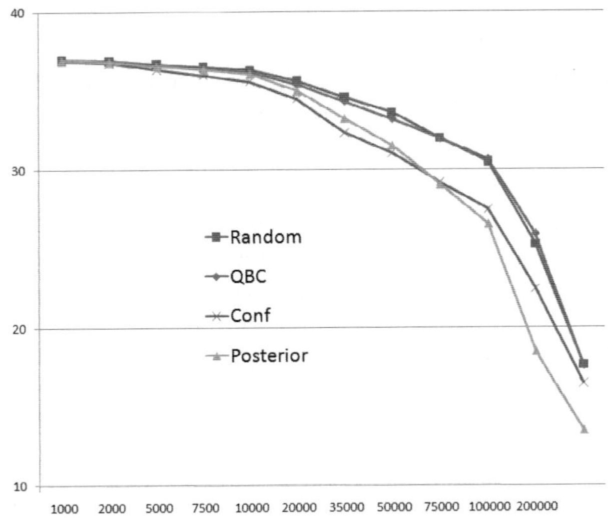

Figure 1: Chinese-English: Link Selection Results

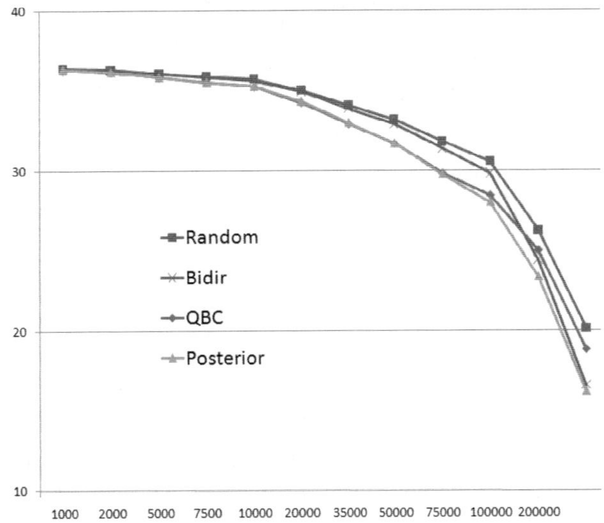

Figure 2: Arabic-English: Link Selection Results

in running our link selection algorithm over the entire alignments to determine the most uncertain links according to each active learning strategy. The links are then looked up in the gold standard human alignment database and corrected. In scenarios where an alignment link is not present in the gold standard data for the source word, we introduce a NULL alignment constraint, else we select all the links as given in the gold standard. The aim of our work is to show that active learning can help in selecting informative alignment links, which if manually labeled can reduce the overall alignment error rate of the given corpus. We, therefore measure the reduction of alignment error rate (AER) of a semi-supervised word aligner that uses this extra information to align the corpus. We plot performance curves for both Chinese-English, Figure 1 and Arabic-English, Figure 2, with number of manual links elicited on x-axis and AER on y-axis. In each iteration of the experiment, we gradually increase the number of links selected from gold standard and make them available to the semi-supervised word aligner and measure the overall reduction of AER on the corpus. We compare our link selection strategies to a baseline approach, where links are selected at random for manual correction.

All our approaches perform equally or better than the baseline for both language pairs. Query by committee (qbc) performs similar to the baseline in Chinese-English and only slightly better for Arabic-English. This could be due to our committee consisting of two alignments that differ only in direction and so are not sufficient in deciding for uncertainty. We will be exploring alternative formulations to this strategy. Confidence based and uncertainty based metrics perform significantly better than the baseline in both language pairs. We can interpret the improvements in two ways. For the same number of manual alignments elicited, our selection strategies select links that provide higher reduction of error when compared to the baseline. An alternative interpretation is that assuming a uniform cost per link, our best selection strategy achieves similar performance to the baseline, at a much lower cost of elicitation.

6.3 Translation Results

We also perform end-to-end machine translation experiments to show that our improvement of alignment quality leads to an improvement of translation scores. For Chinese-English, we train a standard phrase-based SMT system (Koehn et al., 2007) over the available 21,863 sentences. We tune on the MT-Eval 2004 dataset and test on a subset of MT-Eval 2005 dataset consisting of 631 sentences. The language model we use is built using only the English side of the parallel corpus. We understand that this language model is not the optimal choice, but we are interested in testing the word alignment accuracy, which primarily affects the translation model.

Cn-En	BLEU	METEOR
Baseline	18.82	42.70
Human Alignment	19.96	44.22
Active Selection 20%	19.34	43.25

Table 3: Effect of Alignment on Translation Quality

We first obtain the baseline score by training in an unsupervised manner, where no manual alignment is used. We also train a configuration, where we substitute the final word alignment with gold standard manual alignment for the entire parallel corpus. This is an upper bound on the translation accuracy that can be achieved by any alignment link selection algorithm for this dataset. We now take our best link selection criteria, which is the confidence based method and re-train the MT system after eliciting manual information for only 20% of the alignment links. We observe that at this point we have reduced the AER from 37.09 to 26.57. The translation accuracy reported in Table 3, as measured by BLEU (Papineni et al., 2002) and METEOR (Lavie and Agarwal, 2007), also shows significant improvement and approaches the quality achieved using gold standard data. We did not perform MT experiments with Arabic-English dataset due to the incompatibility of tokenization schemes between the manually aligned parallel corpora and publicly available evaluation sets.

7 Conclusion

Word-Alignment is a particularly challenging problem and has been addressed in a completely unsupervised manner thus far (Brown et al., 1993). While generative alignment models have been successful, lack of sufficient data, model assumptions and local optimum during training are well known problems. Semi-supervised techniques use partial manual alignment data to address some of these issues. We have shown that active learning strategies can reduce the effort involved in eliciting human alignment data. The reduction in effort is due to careful selection of maximally uncertain links that provide the most benefit to the alignment model when used in a semi-supervised training fashion. Experiments on Chinese-English have shown considerable improvements.

8 Future Work

In future, we wish to work with word alignments for other language pairs as well as study the effect of manual alignments by varying the size of available parallel data. We also plan to obtain alignments from non-experts over online marketplaces like Amazon Mechanical Turk to further reduce the cost of annotation. We will be experimenting with obtaining full-alignment vs. partial alignment from non-experts. Our hypothesis is that, humans are good at performing tasks of smaller size and so we can extract high quality alignments in the partial alignment case. Cost of link annotation in our current work is assumed to be uniform, but this needs to be revisited. We will also experiment with active learning techniques for identifying sentence pairs with very low alignment confidence, where obtaining full-alignment is equivalent to obtaining multiple partial alignments.

Acknowledgments

This research was partially supported by DARPA under grant NBCHC080097. Any opinions, findings, and conclusions expressed in this paper are those of the authors and do not necessarily reflect the views of the DARPA. The first author would like to thank Qin Gao for the semi-supervised word alignment software and help with running experiments.

References

John Blatz, Erin Fitzgerald, George Foster, Simona Gandrabur, Cyril Goutte, Alex Kulesza, Alberto Sanchis, and Nicola Ueffing. 2004. Confidence estimation for machine translation. In *Proceedings of Coling 2004*, pages 315–321, Geneva, Switzerland, Aug 23–Aug 27. COLING.

Peter F. Brown, Vincent J. Della Pietra, Stephen A. Della Pietra, and Robert L. Mercer. 1993. The mathematics of statistical machine translation: parameter estimation. *Computational Linguistics*, 19(2):263–311.

Chris Callison-Burch, David Talbot, and Miles Osborne. 2004. Statistical machine translation with word- and sentence-aligned parallel corpora. In *ACL 2004*, page 175, Morristown, NJ, USA. Association for Computational Linguistics.

O. Chapelle, B. Schölkopf, and A. Zien, editors. 2006. *Semi-Supervised Learning*. MIT Press, Cambridge, MA.

Colin Cherry and Dekang Lin. 2006. Soft syntactic constraints for word alignment through discriminative training. In *Proceedings of the COLING/ACL on Main conference poster sessions*, pages 105–112, Morristown, NJ, USA.

Pinar Donmez and Jaime G. Carbonell. 2008. Optimizing estimated loss reduction for active sampling in rank learning. In *ICML '08: Proceedings of the 25th international conference on Machine learning*, pages 248–255, New York, NY, USA. ACM.

Alexander Fraser and Daniel Marcu. 2006. Semi-supervised training for statistical word alignment. In *ACL-44: Proceedings of the 21st International Conference on Computational Linguistics and the 44th annual meeting of the Association for Computational Linguistics*, pages 769–776, Morristown, NJ, USA. Association for Computational Linguistics.

Alexander Fraser and Daniel Marcu. 2007. Measuring word alignment quality for statistical machine translation. *Comput. Linguist.*, 33(3):293–303.

Yoav Freund, Sebastian H. Seung, Eli Shamir, and Naftali Tishby. 1997. Selective sampling using the query by committee algorithm. *Machine. Learning.*, 28(2-3):133–168.

Qin Gao and Stephan Vogel. 2008. Parallel implementations of word alignment tool. In *Software Engineering, Testing, and Quality Assurance for Natural Language Processing*, pages 49–57, Columbus, Ohio, June. Association for Computational Linguistics.

Gholamreza Haffari, Maxim Roy, and Anoop Sarkar. 2009. Active learning for statistical phrase-based machine translation. In *Proceedings of HLT NAACL 2009*, pages 415–423, Boulder, Colorado, June. Association for Computational Linguistics.

Fei Huang. 2009. Confidence measure for word alignment. In *Proceedings of the Joint ACL and IJCNLP*, pages 932–940, Suntec, Singapore, August. Association for Computational Linguistics.

Rebecca Hwa. 2004. Sample selection for statistical parsing. *Comput. Linguist.*, 30(3):253–276.

Philipp Koehn, Hieu Hoang, Alexandra Birch Mayne, Christopher Callison-Burch, Marcello Federico, Nicola Bertoldi, Brooke Cowan, Wade Shen, Christine Moran, Richard Zens, Chris Dyer, Ondrej Bojar, Alexandra Constantin, and Evan Herbst. 2007. Moses: Open source toolkit for statistical machine translation. In *ACL Demonstration Session*.

Alon Lavie and Abhaya Agarwal. 2007. Meteor: an automatic metric for mt evaluation with high levels of correlation with human judgments. In *WMT 2007*, pages 228–231, Morristown, NJ, USA.

David D. Lewis and Jason Catlett. 1994. Heterogeneous uncertainty sampling for supervised learning. In *In Proceedings of the Eleventh International Conference on Machine Learning*, pages 148–156. Morgan Kaufmann.

Hieu T. Nguyen and Arnold Smeulders. 2004. Active learning using pre-clustering. In *ICML*.

Franz Josef Och and Hermann Ney. 2003. A systematic comparison of various statistical alignment models. *Computational Linguistics*, pages 19–51.

Kishore Papineni, Salim Roukos, Todd Ward, and Wei-Jing Zhu. 2002. Bleu: a method for automatic evaluation of machine translation. In *ACL 2002*, pages 311–318, Morristown, NJ, USA.

Dan Shen, Jie Zhang, Jian Su, Guodong Zhou, and Chew-Lim Tan. 2004. Multi-criteria-based active learning for named entity recognition. In *ACL '04: Proceedings of the 42nd Annual Meeting on Association for Computational Linguistics*, page 589, Morristown, NJ, USA. Association for Computational Linguistics.

Min Tang, Xiaoqiang Luo, and Salim Roukos. 2001. Active learning for statistical natural language parsing. In *ACL '02*, pages 120–127, Morristown, NJ, USA.

Katrin Tomanek and Udo Hahn. 2009. Semi-supervised active learning for sequence labeling. In *Proceedings of the Joint Conference of the 47th Annual Meeting of the ACL and the 4th International Joint Conference on Natural Language Processing of the AFNLP*, pages 1039–1047, Suntec, Singapore, August. Association for Computational Linguistics.

Simon Tong and Daphne Koller. 2002. Support vector machine active learning with applications to text classification. *Journal of Machine Learning*, pages 45–66.

Gokhan Tur, Dilek Hakkani-Tr, and Robert E. Schapire. 2005. Combining active and semi-supervised learning for spoken language understanding. *Speech Communication*, 45(2):171 – 186.

Nicola Ueffing and Hermann Ney. 2007. Word-level confidence estimation for machine translation. *Comput. Linguist.*, 33(1):9–40.

Hua Wu, Haifeng Wang, and Zhanyi Liu. 2006. Boosting statistical word alignment using labeled and unlabeled data. In *Proceedings of the COLING/ACL on Main conference poster sessions*, pages 913–920, Morristown, NJ, USA. Association for Computational Linguistics.

X. Zhu. 2005. Semi-Supervised Learning Literature Survey. Technical Report 1530, Computer Sciences, University of Wisconsin-Madison. http://www.cs.wisc.edu/~jerryzhu/pub/ssl_survey.pdf.

D-Confidence: an active learning strategy which efficiently identifies small classes

Nuno Escudeiro
Instituto Superior de Engenharia do Porto
Rua Dr António Bernardino de Almeida, 431
Porto, P-4200-072 PORTO, Portugal
LIAAD-INESC PORTO L.A.
Rua de Ceuta, 118 - 6
Porto, P-4050-190 PORTO, Portugal
nfe@isep.ipp.pt

Alípio Jorge
LIAAD-INESC PORTO L.A.
Rua de Ceuta, 118 - 6
Porto, P-4050-190 PORTO, Portugal
amjorge@fc.up.pt

Abstract

In some classification tasks, such as those related to the automatic building and maintenance of text corpora, it is expensive to obtain labeled examples to train a classifier. In such circumstances it is common to have massive corpora where a few examples are labeled (typically a minority) while others are not. Semi-supervised learning techniques try to leverage the intrinsic information in unlabeled examples to improve classification models. However, these techniques assume that the labeled examples cover all the classes to learn which might not stand. In the presence of an imbalanced class distribution getting labeled examples from minority classes might be very costly if queries are randomly selected. Active learning allows asking an oracle to label new examples, that are criteriously selected, and does not assume a previous knowledge of all classes. D-Confidence is an active learning approach that is effective when in presence of imbalanced training sets. In this paper we discuss the performance of d-Confidence over text corpora. We show empirically that d-Confidence reduces the number of queries required to identify examples from all classes to learn when compared to confidence, a common active learning criterion.

1 Introduction

Classification tasks require a number of previously labeled cases. A major bottleneck is that case labeling is a laborious task requiring significant human effort. This effort is particularly high in the case of text documents, web pages and other unstructured objects.

The effort required to retrieve representative labeled examples to learn a classification model is not only related to the number of distinct classes (Adami et al., 2005); it is also related to class distribution in the available pool of examples. On a highly imbalanced class distribution, it is particularly demanding to identify examples from minority classes. These, however, may be important in terms of representativeness. Failing to identify cases from underrepresented classes may have costs. Minority classes may correspond to specific information needs which are relevant for specific subgroups of users. In many situations, such as fraud detection, clinical diagnosis, news (Ribeiro and Escudeiro, 2008) and Web resources (Escudeiro and Jorge, 2006), we face the problem of imbalanced class distributions.

The aim of our current work is to get a classification model that is able to fully recognize the target concept, including all the classes to learn no mater how frequent or rare they are.

Our main goal is to identify representative examples for each class in the absence of previous descriptions of some or all the classes. Furthermore, this must be achieved with a reduced number of labeled examples in order to reduce the labeling effort.

There are several learning schemes available for classification. The supervised setting allows users to specify arbitrary concepts. However, it requires a fully labeled training set, which is prohibitive when the labeling cost is high and, besides that, it requires labeled cases from all classes. Semi-supervised learning allows users to state specific needs without

Proceedings of the NAACL HLT 2010 Workshop on Active Learning for Natural Language Processing, pages 18–26,
Los Angeles, California, June 2010.

requiring extensive labeling (Chapelle et al, 2006) but still requires that labeled examples fully cover the target concept. Unsupervised learning does not require any labeling but users have no chance to tailor clusters to their specific needs and there is no guarantee that the induced clusters are aligned with the classes to learn. In active learning, that seems more adequate to our goals, the learner is allowed to ask an oracle (typically a human) to label examples – these requests are called *queries*. The most informative queries are selected by the learning algorithm instead of being randomly selected as is the case in supervised learning.

In this paper we evaluate the performance of *d-Confidence* (Escudeiro and Jorge, 2009) on text corpora. D-Confidence is an active learning approach that tends to explore unseen regions in case space, thus selecting cases from unseen classes faster – with fewer queries – than traditional active learning approaches. D-Confidence selects queries based on a criterion that aggregates the posterior classifier confidence – a traditional active learning criterion – and the distance between queries and known classes. This criterion is biased towards cases that do not belong to known classes (low confidence) and that are located in unseen areas in case space (high distance to known classes). D-confidence is more effective than confidence alone in achieving an homogeneous coverage of target classes.

In the rest of this paper we start by reviewing active learning, in section 2. Section 3 describes d-Confidence. The evaluation process is presented in section 4 and we state our conclusions and expectations for future work in section 5.

2 Active Learning

Active learning approaches (Angluin, 1988; Cohn et al., 1994; Muslea et al., 2006) reduce label complexity – the number of queries that are necessary and sufficient to learn a concept – by analyzing unlabeled cases and selecting the most useful ones once labeled. Queries may be artificially generated (Baum, 1991) – the *query construction* paradigm – or selected from a pool (Cohn et al., 1990) or a stream of data – the *query filtering* paradigm. Our current work is developed under the query filtering approach.

The general idea in active learning is to estimate the value of labeling one unlabeled case. Query-By-Committee (Seung et al., 1992), for example, uses a set of classifiers – the committee – to identify the case with the highest disagreement. Schohn et al. (2000) worked on active learning for Support Vector Machines (SVM) selecting queries – cases to be labeled – by their proximity to the dividing hyperplane. Their results are, in some cases, better than if all available data is used to train. Cohn et al. (1996) describe an optimal solution for pool-based active learning that selects the case that, once labeled and added to the training set, produces the minimum expected error. This approach, however, requires high computational effort. Previous active learning approaches (providing non-optimal solutions) aim at reducing uncertainty by selecting the next query as the unlabeled example on which the classifier is less confident.

Batch mode active learning – selecting a batch of queries instead of a single one before retraining – is useful when computational time for training is critical. Brinker (2003) proposes a selection strategy, tailored for SVM, that combines closeness to the dividing hyperplane – assuring a reduction in the version space close to one half – with diversity among selected cases – assuring that newly added examples provide additional reduction of version space. Hoi et al. (2006) suggest a new batch mode active learning relying on the Fisher information matrix to ensure small redundancy among selected cases. Li et al. (2006) compute diversity within selected cases from their conditional error.

Dasgupta (2005) defines theoretical bounds showing that active learning has exponentially smaller label complexity than supervised learning under some particular and restrictive constraints. This work is extended in Kaariainen (2006) by relaxing some of these constraints. An important conclusion of this work is that the gains of active learning are much more evident in the initial phase of the learning process, after which these gains degrade and the speed of learning drops to that of passive learning. Agnostic Active learning (Balcan et al., 2006), A^2, achieves an exponential improvement over the usual sample complexity of supervised learning in the presence of arbitrary forms of noise. This model is studied by Hanneke (2007) setting general bounds on label complexity.

All these approaches assume that we have an initial labeled set covering all the classes of interest.

Clustering has also been explored to provide an initial structure to data or to suggest valuable queries. Adami et al. (2005) merge clustering and oracle labeling to bootstrap a predefined hierarchy of classes. Although the original clusters provide some structure to the input, this approach still demands for a high validation effort, especially when these clusters are not aligned with class labels. Dasgupta et al. (2008) propose a cluster-based method that consistently improves label complexity over supervised learning. Their method detects and exploits clusters that are loosely aligned with class labels.

Among other paradigms, it is common that active learning methods select the queries which are closest to the decision boundary of the current classifier. These methods focus on improving the decision functions for the classes that are already known, i.e., those having labeled cases present in the training set. The work presented in this paper diverges classifier attention to other regions increasing the chances of finding new labels.

3 D-Confidence Active Learning

Given a target concept with an arbitrary number of classes together with a sample of unlabeled examples from the target space (the working set), our purpose is to identify representative cases covering all classes while posing as few queries as possible, where a query consists of requesting a label to a specific case. The working set is assumed to be representative of the class space – the representativeness assumption (Liu and Motoda, 2001).

Active learners commonly search for queries in the neighborhood of the decision boundary, where class uncertainty is higher. Limiting case selection to the uncertainty region seems adequate when we have at least one labeled case from each class. This class representativeness is assumed by all active learning methods. In such a scenario, selecting queries from the uncertainty region is very effective in reducing version space.

Nevertheless, our focus is on text corpora where only few labeled examples exist and when we are still looking for exemplary cases to qualify the concept to learn. Under these circumstances – while we do not have labeled cases covering all classes – the uncertainty region, as perceived by the active learner, is just a subset of the real uncertainty region. Being limited to this partial view of the concept, the learner is more likely to waste queries. The amount of the uncertainty region that the learner misses is related to the number of classes to learn that have not yet been identified as well as to the class distribution in the training set.

The intuition behinf d-Confidence is that query selection should be based not only on classifier confidence but also on distance to previously labeled cases. In the presence of two cases with equally low confidence d-Confidence selects the one that is farther apart from what is already know, i.e., from previously labeled cases.

3.1 D-Confidence

Common active learning approaches rely on classifier confidence to select queries (Angluin, 1988) and assume that the pre-labeled set covers all the labels to learn – this assumption does not hold in our scenario. These approaches use the current classification model at each iteration to compute the posterior confidence on each known class for each unlabeled case. Then, they select, as the next query, the unlabeled case with the lowest confidence.

D-Confidence, weighs the confidence of the classifier with the inverse of the distance between the case at hand and previously known classes.

This bias is expected to favor a faster coverage of case space, exhibiting a tendency to explore unknown areas. As a consequence, it provides faster convergence than confidence alone. This drift towards unexplored regions and unknown classes is achieved by selecting the case with the lowest d-Confidence as the next query. Lowest d-Confidence is achieved by combining low confidence – probably indicating cases from unknown classes – with high distance to known classes – pointing to unseen regions in the case space. This effect produces significant differences in the behavior of the learning process. Common active learners focus on the uncertainty region asking queries that are expected to narrow it down. The issue is that the uncertainty region is determined by the labels we known at a given iteration. Focusing our search for queries exclusively

Table 1: d-Confidence algorithm.

(1) given W; L_1 and K
(2) compute distance among cases in W
(3) $i = 1$
(4) while (not stopping criteria) {
(5) $U_i = W - L_i$
(6) learn h_i from L_i
(7) apply hi to Ui generating $conf_i(u_j, c_k)$
(8) for($u_j in U_i$){
(9) $dist_i(u_j, c_k) = aggrIndivDistk(u_i, c_k)$
(10) $dconf_i(u_j, c_k) = \frac{conf_i(u_j, c_k)}{dist_i(u_j, c_k)}$
(11) $dC_i(u_j) = agConf_k(dconf_i(u_j, c_k))$
(12) }
(13) $q_i = u_j : dC_i(u_j) = min_u(dC_i(u))$
(14) $L_{i+1} = L_i \cup < q_i, label(q_i) >$
(15) $i++$
(16) }

on this region, while we are still looking for exemplary cases on some labels that are not yet known, is not effective. Unknown classes hardly come by unless they are represented in the current uncertainty region.

In Table 1 we present the d-Confidence algorithm – an active learning proposal specially tailored to achieve a class representative coverage fast.

W is the working set, a representative sample of cases from the problem space. L_i is a subset of W. Members of L_i are the cases in W whose labels are known at iteration i. U, a subset of W, is the set of unlabeled examples. At iteration i, U_i is the (set) difference between W and L_i; K is the number of target concept classes, c_k; h_i represents the classifier learned at iteration i; q_i is the query at iteration i; C_i is the set of classes known at iteration i – that is the set of distinct classes from all L_i elements; $conf_i(u_j, c_k)$ is the posterior confidence on class c_k given case u_j, at iteration i.

D-Confidence for unlabeled cases is computed at steps (8) to (12) in Table 1 as explained below. In (13) the case with the minimum d-Confidence is selected as the next query. This query is added to the labeled set (14), and removed from the unlabeled pool, and the whole process iterates.

Computing d-Confidence d-Confidence is obtained as the ratio between confidence and distance among cases and known classes (Equation 1).

$$\arg\max_k \left(\frac{conf\,(c_k|u)}{median_j\,(dist\,(u, Xlab_{j,k}))} \right) \quad (1)$$

For a given unlabeled case, u, the classifier generates the posterior confidence w.r.t. known classes (7). Confidence is then divided by an indicator of the distance, $dist()$, between unlabeled case u and all labeled cases belonging to class c_k, $Xlab_{j,k}$ (9). This distance indicator is the $median$ of the distances between case u and all cases in $Xlab_{j,k}$. The median is expected to soften the effect of outliers. At step (10) we compute $dconf_i(u, c_k)$ – the d-Confidence for each known class, c_k, given the case u – by dividing class confidence for a given case by aggregated distance to that class.

Finally, d-Confidence of the case is computed, $dC_i(u)$, as the maximum d-Confidence on individual classes, $agConf_k(conf_i(u, c_k))$, at step (11).

4 Evaluation

D-Confidence was evaluated on two text corpora. We have selected a stratified sample from the 20 Newsgroups (NG) – with 500 documents – and another one from the R52 set of the Reuters-21578 collection (R52) – with 1000 documents. The NG dataset has documents from 20 distinct classes while the R52 dataset has documents from 52 distinct classes. These samples have been selected because they have distinct class distributions.

The class distribution of NG is fairly balanced (Figure 1) with a maximum frequency of 35 and a minimum frequency of 20.

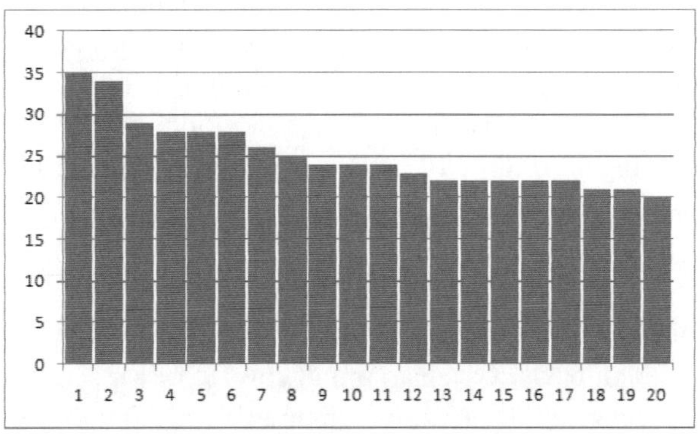

Figure 1: Class distribution in NG dataset

On the other hand, the R52 dataset presents an highly imbalanced class distribution (Figure 2).

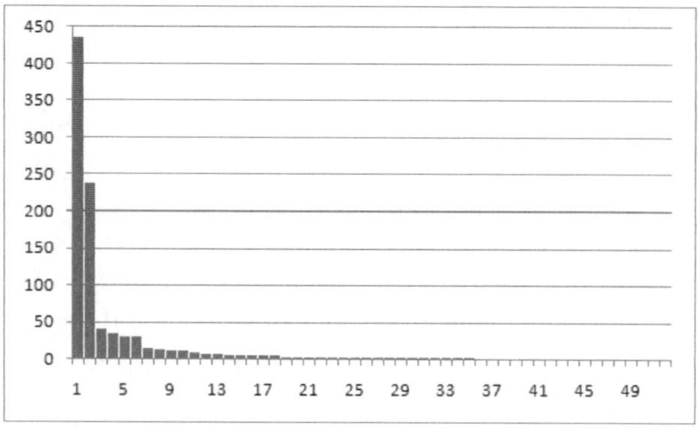

Figure 2: Class distribution in R52 dataset

The most frequent class in R52 has a frequency of 435 while the least frequent has only 2 examples in the dataset. This dataset has 42 classes, out of 52, with a fequency below 10.

4.1 Experimental Setting

We have used Support Vector Machine classifiers (SVM) with linear kernels in all experiments.

In all the experiments we have compared the performance of d-Confidence against confidence – a common active learning setting where query selection is based on low posterior confidence of the current classifier. This comparison is important to evaluate our proposal since d-Confidence is derived from confidence by means of an aggregation with distance in case space. Comparing both these criteria, one against the other, will provide evidence on the performance gains, or losses, of d-Confidence on text when compared to confidence, its baseline.

We have performed 10-fold cross validation on all datasets for standard confidence and d-Confidence active learning. The labels in the training set are hidden from the classifier. In each iteration, the active learning algorithm asks for the label of a single case. For the initial iteration in each fold we give two labeled cases – from two distinct classes – to the classifier. The two initial classes are chosen for each fold, so that different class combinations occur in different folds. Given an initial class to be present in L_1, the specific cases to include in L_1 are randomly sampled from the set of cases on that class. Given the fold, the same L_1 is used for all experiments.

4.2 Results

Our experiments assess the ability of d-Confidence to reduce the labeling effort when compared to confidence.

We have recorded, for each dataset, the number of distinct labels already identified and the progress of the error on the test set for each iteration (generalization error). From these, we have computed, for each dataset, the mean number of known classes and mean generalization error in each iteration over all the cross validation folds (Figures 3 and 4).

The chart legends use *c* for confidence, *dc* for d-Confidence, *e* for generalization error and *kc* for the number of known classes. For convenience of representation the number of classes that are known at each iteration has been normalized to the total number of classes in the dataset thus being transformed into the percentage of known classes instead of the absolute number of known classes. This way the number of known classes and generalization error are both bounded in the same range (between 0 and 1) and we can conveniently represented them in the same chart.

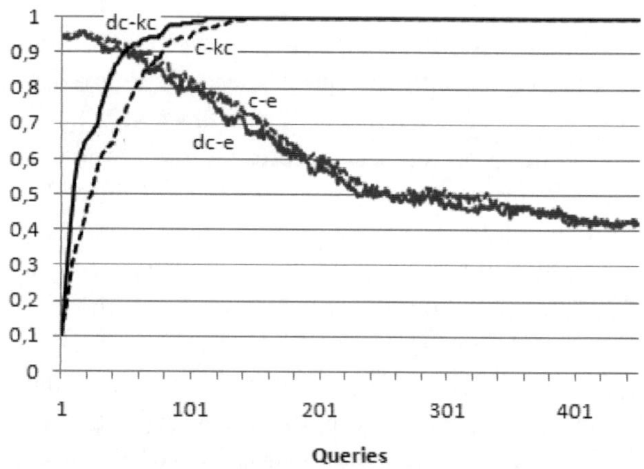

Figure 3: Known classes and error in NG dataset

Means are micro-averages – all the cases are equally weighted – over all iterations for a given dataset and a given selection criterion (confidence or d-Confidence). Besides the overall number of queries required to retrieve labels from all classes and generalization error, we have also observed the mean number of queries that are required to retrieve the first case for each class (Tables 2 to 4) – referred to as *first hit*.

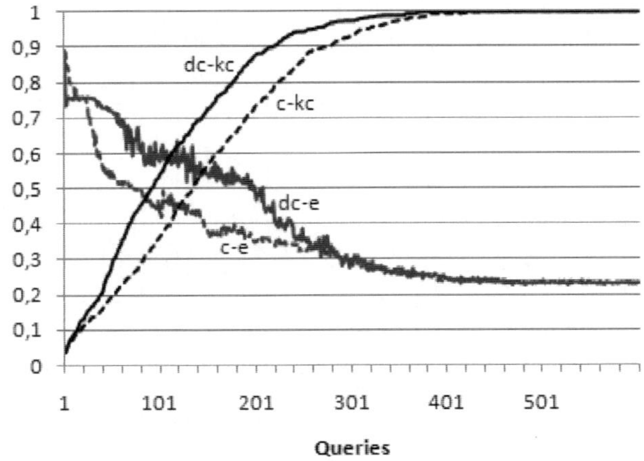

Figure 4: Known classes and error in R52 dataset

We have performed significance tests, t-tests, for the differences of the means observed when using confidence and d-Confidence. Statistically different means, at a significance level of 5%, are bold faced.

When computing first hit for a given class we have omitted the experiments where the labeled set for the first iteration contains cases from that class. Figures 5 and 6 give an overview of the number of queries that are required in each setting to first hit a given number of distinct classes.

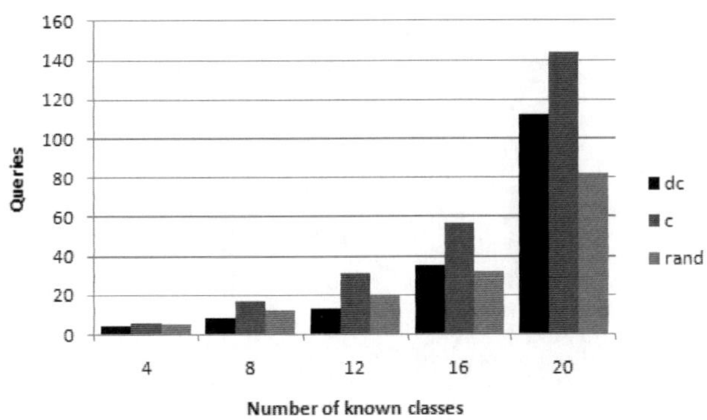

Figure 5: Queries required to identify bunches of distinct classes in NG dataset

A benchmark based on random selection is also provided – averaged over 10 random samples. We have recorded the number of queries required to identify bunches of distinct classes in multiples of 10 for R52 and multiples of 4 in NG.

Table 2: Class distribution (freq) and first hit (c-fh and dc-fh) for the NG dataset.

Class	Freq	c-fh	dc-fh
1	29	36.9	35.7
2	22	41.9	41.1
3	21	**57.3**	76.9
4	34	23.5	**5.9**
5	35	18.9	20.2
6	24	37.1	**15.4**
7	21	53.6	**11.3**
8	24	32.9	**13.1**
9	25	36.3	**9.1**
10	22	**41.1**	48.9
11	22	42.5	**3.5**
12	24	28.6	**4.3**
13	28	18.8	20.4
14	28	25.8	**5.4**
15	22	27.4	**6.2**
16	28	14.9	**2.6**
17	23	**21.4**	27.9
18	26	34.5	**7.7**
19	22	22.2	21.2
20	20	26.7	**6.9**
mean		32.1	19.2

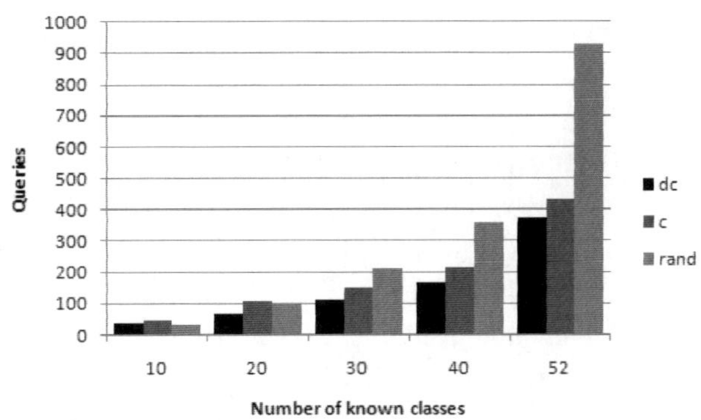

Figure 6: Queries required to identify bunches of distinct classes in R52 dataset

Table 3: Class distribution (Freq) and first hit (c-fh and dc-fh) for the R52 dataset. Only for those classes where d-Confidence outperforms confidence with statistical significance at 5% significance level.

Class	Freq	c-fh	dc-fh
1	239	10.1	**1.6**
2	5	7.2	**1.3**
8	3	103.8	**76.6**
9	7	68.6	**6.6**
10	2	80.0	**10.0**
11	40	83.4	**41.7**
14	2	173.7	**110.6**
15	3	115.6	**64.7**
16	7	96.7	**16.8**
18	5	68.7	**62.9**
22	2	244.4	**197.6**
23	30	153.4	**36.7**
25	4	173.3	**102.9**
26	2	214.1	**123.9**
27	5	206.7	**184.9**
28	2	213.3	**85.2**
29	2	137.6	**44.8**
30	3	159.3	**52.1**
31	2	159.1	**144.8**
32	2	179.7	**123.9**
33	30	160.8	**76.1**
34	15	175.6	**108.7**
36	2	167.4	**107.8**
37	3	118.0	**99.5**
40	2	140.0	**104.7**
43	4	313.1	**256.4**
44	14	216.3	**144.5**
46	12	206	**126.7**
47	2	233.7	**167**
48	3	153.2	**84.1**
49	35	226	**106.9**
50	3	144.3	**75.5**
51	3	148.5	**51.1**
52	2	258.8	**196.5**
mean		156.2	94.0

Table 4: Class distribution (Freq) and first hit (c-fh and dc-fh) for the R52 dataset. Only for those classes where d-Confidence does not outperforms confidence.

Class	Freq	c-fh	dc-fh
3	3	**11.2**	18.0
4	2	**36.4**	72.9
5	6	**23.1**	50.7
6	11	**39.7**	49.7
7	4	**40.1**	89.1
12	2	**128.8**	136.0
13	435	**91.9**	107.8
17	9	**117.0**	135.6
19	2	**123.6**	19.1
20	3	171.7	171.1
21	2	**196.2**	224.0
24	4	**118.6**	178.7
35	4	**146.1**	183.5
38	3	**158.5**	166.4
39	2	152.2	150.4
41	5	**143.6**	154.5
42	3	**188.9**	202.8
45	3	**175.5**	198.7
mean		114.6	128.3

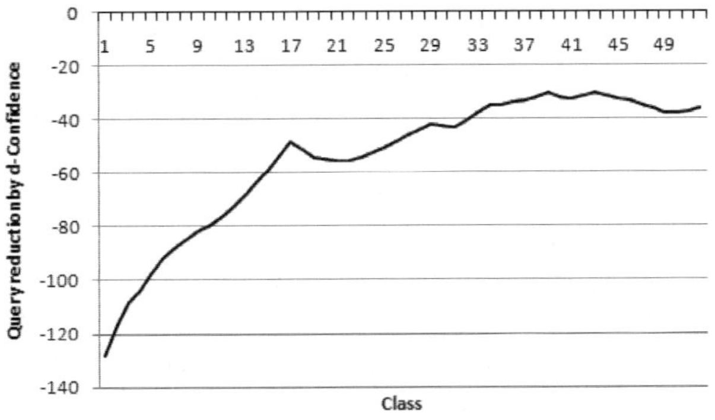

Figure 7: Average gain of d-Confidence to confidence. Classes are sorted by increasing order of their frequency.

4.3 Discussion

The charts in Figures 3 and 4 confirm the results that have been previously reported for standard non-textual datasets (Escudeiro and Jorge, 2009), w.r.t. identification of cases from unknown classes, i.e., d-Confidence reduces the labeling effort that is required to identify examples from all classes. However, the error rate gets worse in the R52 dataset. D-Confidence gets to know more classes from the target concept earlier although less sharply. In the R52 dataset we are exchanging accuracy by representativeness. This might be desirable or not, depending on the specifc task we are dealing with. If we are trying to learn a target concept but we do not know examples from all the classes to learn – for instance if we are in the early stage of a classification problem – this effect might be desirable so we can get a full specification of the target concept with a reduced labeling effort.

It is interesting to notice that d-Confidence outperforms confidence to a greater extent on minority classes. This is obvious in R52 if we compute the cumulative average of the gain in labeling effort that is provided by d-Confidence when compared to confidence (Figure 7).

The gain for each class is defined as the number of queries required by d-Confidence to first hit the class minus the ones that are required by confidence. To compute the moving average, these gains are sorted in increasing order of the class frequency. The average gain starts at -128, for a class with frequency 2, and decreases to the overall average of -36 as class frequency increases up to 435. The bigger gains are observed in the minority classes. Although not as obvious as in R52 this same behaviour is also observed in the NG dataset.

Figures 5 and 6, as well as Tables 2 to 4, show that d-Confidence reduces the labeling effort required to identify unknown classes when compared to confidence. When selecting cases to label randomly, the first bunch of 10 distinct classes is found as fast as with d-Confidence but, from there on, when rare classes come by, d-Confidence takes the lead. The outcome is quite different in the NG dataset. In this dataset d-Confidence still outperforms confidence but it is beaten by random selection of cases after identifying 13.3 classes on average (after 22 queries on average). This observation led us to suspect that when in presence of balanced datasets, d-Confidence identifies new classes faster than random selection in the initial phase of the learning process but selecting cases by chance is better to identify cases in the latest stage of collecting exemplary cases, when few classes remain undetected.

5 Conclusions and Future Work

The evaluation procedure that we have performed provided statistical evidence on the performance of d-Confidence over text corpora when compared to confidence. Although the evaluation has been performed only on two datasets, the conclusions we have reached point out some interesting results.

D-Confidence reduces the labeling effort and identifies exemplary cases for all classes faster that confidence. This gain is bigger for minority classes, which are the ones where the benefits are more relevant.

D-Confidence performs better in imbalanced datasets where it provides significant gains that greatly reduce the labeling effort. For balanced datasets, d-Confidence seems to be valuable in the early stage of the classification task, when few classes are known. In the later stages, random selection of cases seems faster in identifying the few missing classes. However, d-Confidence consistently outperforms confidence.

The main drawback of d-Confidence when applied on imbalanced text corpora is that the reduction in the labeling effort that is achieved in identifying unknown classes is obtained at the cost of increasing error. This increase in error is probably due to the fact that we are diverting the classifier from focusing on the decision function of the majority classes to focus on finding new, minority, classes. As a consequence the classification model generated by d-Confidence is able of identifying more distinct classes faster but gets less sharp in each one of them. This is particularly harmful for accuracy since a more fuzzy decision boundary for majority classes might cause many erroneous guesses with a negative impact on error.

We are now exploring semi-supervised learning to leverage the intrinsic value of unlabeled cases so we can benefit from the reduction in labeling effort provided by d-Confidence without increasing error.

6 References

G. Adami, P. Avesani, and D. Sona. Clustering documents into a web directory for bootstrapping a supervised classification. Data and Knowledge Engineering, 54:301325, 2005.

D. Angluin. Queries and concept learning. Machine Learning, 2:319342, 1988.

M.-F. Balcan, A. Beygelzimer, and J. Langford. Agnostic active learning. In In ICML, pages 6572. ICML, 2006.

E. Baum. Neural net algorithms that learn in polynomial time from examples and queries. IEEE Transactions in Neural Networks, 2:519, 1991.

K. Brinker. Incorporating diversity in active learning with support vector machines. In Proceedings of the Twentieth International Conference on Machine Learning, 2003.

O. Chapelle, B. Schoelkopf and A. Zien (Eds). Semi-supervised Learning. MIT Press, Cambridge, MA, 2006.

D. Cohn, L. Atlas, and R. Ladner. Training connectionist networks with queries and selective sampling. In Advances in Neural Information Processing Systems, 1990.

D. Cohn, L. Atlas, and R. Ladner. Improving generalization with active learning. Machine Learning, (15):201221, 1994.

D. Cohn, Z. Ghahramani, and M. Jordan. Active learning with statistical models. Journal of Artificial Intelligence Research, 4:129145, 1996.

S. Dasgupta. Coarse sample complexity bonds for active learning. In Advances in Neural Information Processing Systems 18. 2005.

S. Dasgupta and D. Hsu. Hierarchical sampling for active learning. In Proceedings of the 25th International Conference on Machine Learning, 2008.

N. Escudeiro and A.M. Jorge. Efficient coverage of case space with active learning. In P. M. L. M. R. Lus Seabra Lopes, Nuno Lau, editor, Progress in Artificial Intelligence, Proceedings of the 14th Portuguese Conference on Artificial Intelligence (EPIA 2009), volume 5816, pages 411422. Springer, 2009.

S. Hanneke. A bound on the label complexity of agnostic active learning. In Proceedings of the 24th International Conference on Machine Learning, 2007.

S. Hoi, R. Jin, and M. Lyu. Large-scale text categorization by batch mode active learning. In Proceedings of the World Wide Web Conference, 2006.

M. Kaariainen. Algorithmic Learning Theory, chapter Active learning in the non-realizable case, pages 63 77. Springer Berlin / Heidelberg, 2006.

M. Li and I. Sethi. Confidence-based active learning. IEEE Transactions on Pattern Analysis and Machine Intelligence, 28:12511261, 2006.

H. Liu and H. Motoda. Instance Selection and Construction for Data Mining. Kluver Academic Publishers, 2001.

I. Muslea, S. Minton, and C. A. Knoblock. Active learning with multiple views. Journal of Artificial Intelligence Research, 27:203233, 2006.

P. Ribeiro and N. Escudeiro. On-line news ‘a la carte. In Proceedings of the European Conference on the Use of Modern Information and Communication Technologies, 2008.

N. Roy and A. McCallum. Toward optimal active learning through sampling estimation of error reduction. In Proceedings of the International Conference on Machine Learning, 2001.

G. Schohn and D. Cohn. Less is more: Active learning with support vector machines. In Proceedings of the International Conference on Machine Learning, 2000.

H. Seung, M. Opper, and H. Sompolinsky. Query by committee. In Proceedings of the 5th Annual Workshop on Computational Learning Theory, 1992.

Domain Adaptation meets Active Learning

Piyush Rai, Avishek Saha, Hal Daumé III, and Suresh Venkatasubramanian
School of Computing, University of Utah
Salt Lake City, UT 84112
{piyush,avishek,hal,suresh}@cs.utah.edu

Abstract

In this work, we show how active learning in some (target) domain can leverage information from a different but related (source) domain. We present an algorithm that harnesses the source domain data to learn the best possible initializer hypothesis for doing active learning in the target domain, resulting in improved label complexity. We also present a variant of this algorithm which additionally uses the domain divergence information to selectively query the most informative points in the target domain, leading to further reductions in label complexity. Experimental results on a variety of datasets establish the efficacy of the proposed methods.

1 Introduction

Acquiring labeled data to train supervised learning models can be difficult or expensive in many problem domains. Active Learning tries to circumvent this difficultly by only querying the labels of the most informative examples and, in several cases, has been shown to achieve exponentially lower label-complexity (number of queried labels) than supervised learning (Cohn et al., 1994). Domain Adaptation (Daumé & Marcu, 2006), although motivated somewhat differently, attempts to address a seemingly similar problem: lack of labeled data in some target domain. Domain Adaptation deals with this problem using labeled data from a different (but related) *source* domain.

In this paper, we consider the *supervised* domain adaptation setting (Finkel & Manning, 2009; Daumé III, 2007) having a large amount of labeled data from a source domain, a large amount of unlabeled data from a target domain, and *additionally* a small budget for acquiring labels in the target domain. We show how, apart from leveraging information in the usual domain adaptation sense, the information from the source domain can be leveraged to intelligently query labels in the target domain.We achieve this by first training the best possible classifier *without* using target domain labeled data [1] and then using the learned classifier to leverage the inter-domain information when we are additionally provided some fixed budget for acquiring extra *labeled* target data (i.e., the active learning setting (Settles, 2009)).

There are several ways in which our "best classifier" can be utilized. Our first approach uses this classifier as the initializer while doing (online) active learning in the target domain (Section 3). Then we present a variant augmenting the first approach using a domain-separator hypothesis which leads to *additionally* ruling out querying the labels of those target examples that appear "similar" to the source domain (Section 4).

Figure 1 shows our basic setup which uses a source (or unsupervised domain-adapted source) classifier $\mathbf{v}_0$ as an initializer for doing active learning in the target domain having some small, fixed budget for querying labels. Our framework consists of 2 phases: 1) Learning the best possible classi-

[1] For instance, either by simply training a supervised classifier on the labeled source data, or by using *unsupervised* domain adaptation techniques (Blitzer et al., 2006; Sugiyama et al., 2007) that use labeled data from the source domain, and additionally *unlabeled* data from the source and target domains.

Proceedings of the NAACL HLT 2010 Workshop on Active Learning for Natural Language Processing, pages 27–32,
Los Angeles, California, June 2010.

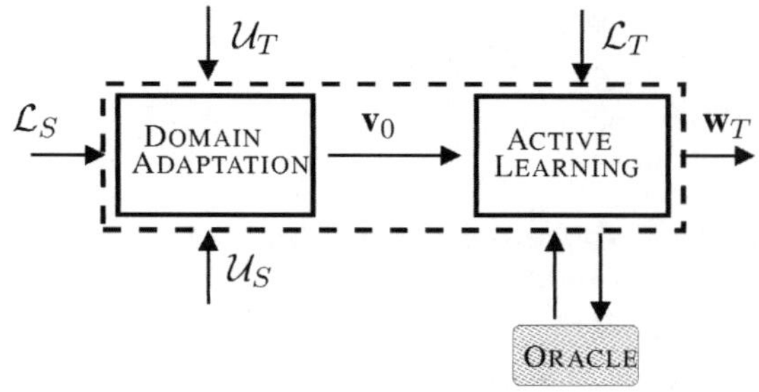

Figure 1: Block diagram of our basic approach. Stage-1 can use any black-box unsupervised domain adaptation approach (e.g., (Blitzer et al., 2006; Sugiyama et al., 2007))

fier $\mathbf{v}_0$ using source labeled ($\mathcal{L}_S$) and unlabeled data ($\mathcal{U}_S$), and target unlabeled ($\mathcal{U}_T$) data, and 2) Querying labels for target domain examples by leveraging information from the classifier learned in phase-1.

2 Online Active Learning

The active learning phase of our algorithm is based on (Cesa-Bianchi et al., 2006), henceforth referred to as CBGZ. In this section, we briefly describe this approach for the sake of completeness.

Their algorithm (Algorithm 1) starts with a zero initialized weight vector $\mathbf{w}_T^0$ and proceeds in rounds by querying the label of an example x_i with probability $\frac{b}{b+|r_i|}$, where $|r_i|$ is the *confidence* (in terms of margin) of the current weight vector on x_i. b is a parameter specifying how aggressively the labels are queried. A large value of b implies that a large number of labels will be queried (conservative sampling) whereas a small value would lead to a small number of examples being queried. For each label queried, the algorithm updates the current weight vector if the label was predicted incorrectly. It is easy to see that the total number of labels queried by this algorithm is $\sum_{i=1}^{T} \mathbb{E}[\frac{b}{b+|r_i|}]$.

3 Active Online Domain Adaptation

In our supervised domain adaptation setting, we are given a small budget for acquiring labels in a target domain, which makes it imperative to use active learning in the target domain. However, our goal is to *additionally* also leverage inter-domain relatedness by exploiting whatever information we might already have from the source domain. To accomplish this, we take the online active learning approach of (Cesa-Bianchi et al., 2006) described in Section 2 and adapt it such that the algorithm uses the best possible classifier learned (*without* target labeled data; see Figure 1) as the initializer hypothesis in the target domain, and thereafter updates this hypothesis in an online fashion using actively acquired labels as is done in (Cesa-Bianchi et al., 2006). This amounts to using $\mathbf{w}_T^0 = \mathbf{v}_0$ in Algorithm 1. We refer to this algorithm as Active Online Domain Adaptation (AODA). It can be shown that the modified algorithm (AODA) yields smaller mistake bound and smaller label complexity than the CBGZ algorithm. We skip the proofs here and reserve the presentation for a longer version. It is however possible to provide an intuitive argument for the smaller label complexity: Since AODA is initialized with a non-zero (*but not randomly chosen*) hypothesis $\mathbf{v}_0$ learned using data from a related source domain, the sequence of hypotheses AODA produces are expected to have higher confidences margins $|r'_i|$ as compared that of CBGZ which is based on a *zero initialized hypothesis*. Therefore, at each round, the sampling probability of AODA given by $\frac{b}{b+|r'_i|}$ will also be smaller, leading to a smaller number of queried labels since it is nothing but $\sum_{i=1}^{T} \mathbb{E}[\frac{b}{b+|r'_i|}]$.

Algorithm 1 CBGZ

Input: $b > 0$; T: number of rounds
Initialization: $\mathbf{w}_T^0 = 0$; $k = 1$;
for $i = 1$ to T **do**
  $\hat{x}_i = x_i/||x_i||$, set $r_i = \mathbf{w}_T^{i-1}\hat{x}_i$;
  predict $\hat{y}_i = SIGN(r_i)$;
  sample $Z_i \sim Bernoulli(\frac{b}{b+|r_i|})$;
  if $Z_i = 1$ **then**
    query label $y_i \in \{+1, -1\}$
    if $\hat{y}_i \neq y_i$ **then**
      update: $\mathbf{w}_T^k = \mathbf{w}_T^{k-1} + y_i\hat{x}_i$; $k \leftarrow k + 1$;
    end if
  end if
end for

4 Using Domain Separator Hypothesis

The relatedness of source and target domains can be additionally leveraged to *further* improve the algorithm described in Section 3. Since the source and target domains are assumed to be related, one can use this fact to upfront rule out acquiring the labels of some target domain examples that “appear” to be similar to the source domain examples. As an illustration, Fig. 2 shows a typical distribution separator hypothesis (Blitzer et al., 2007a) which separates the *source* and *target* examples. If the source and target domains are reasonably different, then the separator hypothesis can perfectly distinguish between the examples drawn from these two domains. On the other hand, if the domains are similar, one would expected that there will be some overlap and therefore some of the target domain examples will lie on the source side (cf., Fig. 2). Acquiring labels for such examples is not really needed since the initializing hypothesis $\mathbf{v}_0$ (cf., Fig 1) of AODA would already have taken into account such examples. Therefore, such target examples can be outrightly ignored from being queried for labels. Our second algorithm (Algorithm 2) is similar to Algorithm 1, but also makes use of the distribution separator hypothesis (which can be learned using source and target *unlabeled* examples) as a preprocessing step before doing active learning on each incoming target example. We denote this algorithm by DS-AODA (for Domain-Separator based AODA). Since some of the target examples are upfront ruled out from being queried, this approach resulted even smaller number of queried labels (Section 5.4).

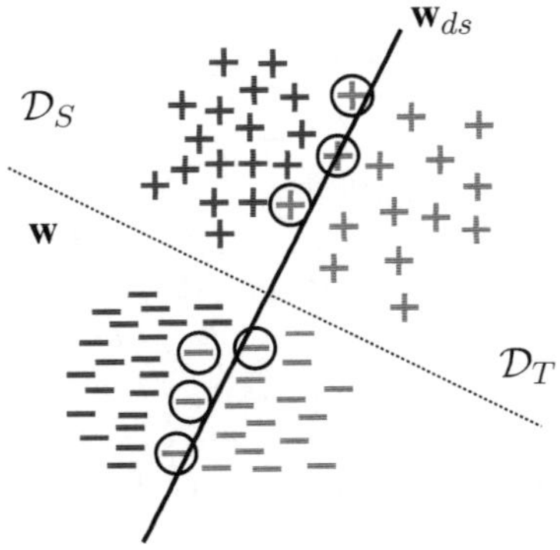

Figure 2: An illustrative diagram showing distribution separator hypothesis $\mathbf{w}_{ds}$ separating source data from target data. $\mathbf{w}$ is the actual target hypothesis

5 Experiments

In this section, we demonstrate the empirical performance of our algorithms and compare them with a

Algorithm 2 DS-AODA

Input: $b > 0$; $\mathbf{w}_{ds}$: distribution separator hypothesis; $\mathbf{v}_0$: initializing hypothesis ; T: number of rounds
Initialization: $\mathbf{w}_T^0 = \mathbf{v}_0$; $k = 1$;
for $i = 1$ to T **do**
  $\hat{x}_i = x_i/||x_i||$,
  if $\hat{x}_i$ does not lie on the source side of $\mathbf{w}'_{ds}$ **then**
    set $r_i = \mathbf{w}_T^{i-1}\hat{x}_i$;
    predict $\hat{y}_i = SIGN(r_i)$;
    sample $Z_i \sim Bernoulli(\frac{b}{b+|r_i|})$;
    if $Z_i = 1$ **then**
      query label $y_i \in \{+1, -1\}$
      if $\hat{y}_i \neq y_i$ **then**
        update: $\mathbf{w}_T^k = \mathbf{w}_T^{k-1} + y_i\hat{x}_i$; $k \leftarrow k+1$;
      end if
    end if
  end if
end for

number of baselines. Table 1 summarizes the methods used with a brief description of each. Among the first three (ID, SDA, FEDA), FEDA (Daumé III, 2007) is a state-of-the-art *supervised* domain adaptation method but assumes *passively* acquired labels. The last four, RIAL, ZIAL, SIAL and AODA methods in Table 1 acquire labels in an active fashion. As the description denotes, RIAL and ZIAL start active learning in *target* with a randomly initialized and zero initialized base hypothesis, respectively. It is also important to distinguish between SIAL and AODA here: SIAL uses an unmodified classifier learned only from *source* labeled data as the initializer, whereas AODA uses an *unsupervised* domain-adaptation technique (i.e., without using labeled target data) to learn the initializer. In our experiments, we use the instance reweighting approach (Sugiyama et al., 2007) to perform the unsupervised domain adaptation step. However, we note that this step can also be performed using any other unsupervised domain adaptation technique such as Structural Correspondence Learning (SCL) (Blitzer et al., 2006). We compare all the approaches based on classification accuracies achieved for a given budget of labeled target examples (Section-5.2), and number of labels requested for a fixed pool of unlabeled target examples and corresponding accuracies

Method	Summary	Active ?
ID	In-domain ($\mathcal{D}_\mathcal{T}$) data	No
sDA	uDA followed by *passively* chosen labeled target data	No
FEDA	Frustratingly Easy Domain Adaptation Daumé III (2007)	No
ZIAL	Zero initialized active learning Cesa-Bianchi et al. (2006)	Yes
RIAL	Randomly initialized active learning with fixed label budget	Yes
SIAL	Source hypothesis initialized active learning	Yes
AODA	uDA based source hypothesis initialized active learning	Yes

Table 1: Description of the methods compared

(Section-5.3). We use the vanilla Perceptron as the base classifier of each of the algorithms and each experiment has been averaged over 20 runs corresponding to random data order permutations.

5.1 Datasets

We report our empirical results for the task of sentiment classification using data provided by (Blitzer et al., 2007b) which consists of user reviews of eight product types (apparel, books, DVD, electronics, kitchen, music, video, and other) from Amazon.com. We also apply PCA to reduce the data-dimensionality to 50. The sentiment classification task for this dataset is binary classification which corresponds to classifying a review as positive or negative. The sentiment dataset consists of several domain pairs with varying $\mathcal{A}$-distance (which measures the domain separation), akin to the sense described in (Ben-David et al., 2006). Table 2 presents the domain pairs used in our experiments and their corresponding domain divergences in terms of the $\mathcal{A}$-distance (Ben-David et al., 2006).

To compute the $\mathcal{A}$-distance from finite samples of source and target domain, we use a surrogate to the true $\mathcal{A}$-distance (the *proxy* $\mathcal{A}$-distance) in a manner similar to (Ben-David et al., 2006): First, we train a linear classifier to separate the *source* domain from the *target* domain using only unlabeled examples from both. The average per-instance hinge-loss of this classifier subtracted from 1 serves as our estimate of the *proxy* $\mathcal{A}$-distance. A score of 1 means perfectly separable distributions whereas a score of 0 means that the two distributions are essentially the same. As a general rule, a high score means that the two domains are reasonably far apart.

Source	Target	$\mathcal{A}$-distance
Dvd (D)	Book (B)	0.7616
Dvd (D)	Music (M)	0.7314
Books (B)	Apparel (A)	0.5970
Dvd (D)	Apparel (A)	0.5778
Electronics (E)	Apparel (A)	0.1717
Kitchen (K)	Apparel (A)	0.0459

Table 2: Proxy $\mathcal{A}$-distances between some domain pairs

5.2 Classification Accuracies

In our first experiment, we compare our first approach of Section 3 (AODA, and also SIAL which naïvely uses the *unadapted* source hypothesis) against other baselines on two domain pairs from the sentiments dataset: DVD→BOOKS (large $\mathcal{A}$ distance) and KITCHEN→APPAREL (small $\mathcal{A}$ distance) with varying target budget (1000 to 5000). The results are shown in Table 3 and Table 4. As the results indicate, on both datasets, our approaches (SIAL, AODA) perform consistently better than the baseline approaches (Table 1) which also include one of the state-of-the-art supervised domain adaptation algorithms (Daumé III, 2007). On the other hand, we observe that the zero-initialized and randomly initialized approaches do not perform as well. In particular, the latter case suggests that it's important to have a sensible initialization.

5.3 Label Complexity Results

Next, we compare the various algorithms on the basis of the number of labels acquired (and corresponding accuracies) when given the complete pool of unlabeled examples from the target domain. Table 5 shows that our approaches result in much smaller label complexities as compared to other ac-

Met-hod	Target Budget 1000	2000	3000	4000	5000
	Acc (Std)	Acc (Std)	Acc (Std)	Acc (Std)	Acc (Std)
ID	65.94 (±3.40)	66.66 (±3.01)	67.00 (±2.40)	65.72 (±3.98)	66.25 (±3.18)
sDA	66.17 (±2.57)	66.45 (±2.88)	65.31 (±3.13)	66.33 (±3.51)	66.22 (±3.05)
RIAL	51.79 (±4.36)	53.12 (±4.65)	55.01 (±4.20)	57.56 (±4.18)	58.57 (±2.44)
ZIAL	66.24 (±3.16)	66.72 (±3.30)	63.97 (±4.82)	66.28 (±3.61)	66.36 (±2.82)
SIAL	**68.22 (±2.17)**	**69.65 (±1.20)**	**69.95 (±1.55)**	70.54 (±1.42)	**70.97 (±0.97)**
AODA	67.64 (±2.35)	68.89 (±1.37)	69.49 (±1.63)	**70.55 (1.15)**	70.65 (±0.94)
FEDA	67.31 (±3.36)	68.47 (±3.15)	68.37 (±2.72)	66.95 (3.11)	67.13 (±3.16)
Acc: Accuracy | **Std:** Standard Deviation					

Table 3: Classification accuracies for DVD→BOOKS, for fixed target budget.

Met-hod	Target Budget 1000	2000	3000	4000	5000
	Acc (Std)	Acc (Std)	Acc (Std)	Acc (Std)	Acc (Std)
ID	69.64 (±3.14)	69.61 (±3.17)	69.36 (±3.14)	69.77 (±3.58)	70.77 (±3.05)
sDA	69.70 (±2.57)	70.48 (±3.42)	70.29 (±2.56)	70.86 (±3.16)	70.71 (±3.65)
RIAL	52.13 (±5.44)	56.83 (±5.36)	58.09 (±4.09)	59.82 (±4.16)	62.03 (±2.52)
ZIAL	70.09 (±3.74)	69.96 (±3.27)	68.6 (±3.94)	70.06 (±2.84)	69.75 (±3.26)
SIAL	73.82 (±1.47)	**74.45 (±1.27)**	75.11 (±0.98)	75.35 (±1.30)	75.58 (±0.85)
AODA	**73.93 (±1.84)**	74.18 (±1.85)	**75.13 (±1.18)**	**75.88 (±1.32)**	**76.02 (±0.97)**
FEDA	70.05 (±2.47)	69.34 (±3.50)	71.22 (±3.00)	71.67 (±2.59)	70.80 (±3.89)
Acc: Accuracy | **Std:** Standard Deviation					

Table 4: Classification accuracies for KITCHEN→APPAREL, for fixed target budget.

tive learning based baselines and still gives better classification accuracies. We also note that although RIAL initializes with a non-zero hypothesis and queries almost similar number of labels as our algorithms, it actually performs worse than even ZIAL in terms of classification accuracies, which implies the significant of a sensible initializing hypothesis.

Met-hod	DVD→BOOK		KITCHEN→APPAREL	
	Acc (Std)	Labels	Acc (Std)	Labels
RIAL	62.74 (±3.00)	7618	62.15 (±4.51)	4871
ZIAL	65.65 (±2.82)	10459	70.19 (±2.64)	6968
SIAL	72.11 (±1.20)	7517	75.62 (±1.14)	**4709**
AODA	72.00 (±1.31)	**7452**	75.62 (±0.82)	4752
Acc: Accuracy | **Std:** Standard Deviation				

Table 5: Accuracy and label complexity of DVD→BOOKS and KITCHEN→APPAREL *with full target training data treated as the unlabeled pool.*

5.4 DS-AODA Results

Finally, we evaluate our distribution separator hypothesis based approach (DS-AODA) discussed in Section 4. As our experimental results (on four domain pairs, Fig. 3) indicate, this approach leads to considerably smaller number of labels acquired than our first approach AODA which does not use the information about domain separation, without any perceptible loss in classification accuracies. Similar improvements in label complexity (although not reported here) were observed when we grafted the distribution separator hypothesis around SIAL (the unaltered source initialized hypothesis).

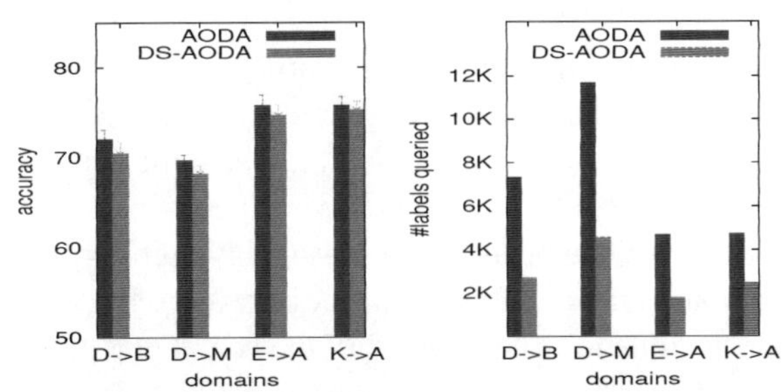

Figure 3: Test accuracy and label complexity of D→B, D→M, E→A and K→A.

5.5 SIAL vs AODA

Some of the results might indicate from naïvely initializing using even the unadapted source trained classifier (SIAL) tends to be as good as initializing with a classifer trained using unsupervised domain adaptation (AODA). However, it is mainly due to the particular unsupervised domain adaptation technique (naïve instance weighting) we have used here for the first stage. In some cases, the weights estimated using instance weighting may not be accurate and the bias in importance weight estimation is potentially the reason behind AODA not doing better than SIAL in such cases. As mentioned earlier, however, any other unsupervised domain adaptation technique can be used here and, in general, AODA is expected to perform better than SIAL.

6 Related Work

Active learning in a domain adaptation setting has received little attention so far. One interesting setting was proposed in (Chan & Ng, 2007) where they apply active learning for word sense disambiguation in a domain adaptation setting. Their active learning setting is pool-based whereas ours is a streaming (online) setting. Furthermore, our second algorithm also uses the domain separator hypothesis to rule out querying the labels of target examples similar to the source. A combination of transfer learning with active learning has been presented in (Shi et al., 2008). One drawback of their approach is the requirement of an initial pool of labeled target domain data used to train an in-domain classifier. Without this in-domain classifier, no transfer learning is possible in their setting.

7 Discussion

There are several interesting variants of our approach that can worth investigating. For instance, one can use a hybrid oracle setting where the source classifier $\mathbf{v}_0$ could be used as an oracle that provides labels for free, whenever it is reasonably highly confident about its prediction (maybe in terms of its relative confidence as compared to the actual classifier being learned; it would also be interesting to set, and possibly adapt, this confidence measure as the active learning progresses). Besides, in the distribution separator hypothesis based approach of Section 4, we empirically observed significant reductions in label-complexity, and it is supported by intuitive arguments. However, it would be interesting to be able to precisely quantify the amount by which the label-complexity is expected to reduce.

References

Ben-David, S., Blitzer, J., Crammer, K., and Pereira, F. Analysis of Representations for Domain Adaptation. In *NIPS*, 2006.

Blitzer, J., Mcdonald, R., and Pereira, F. Domain Adaptation with Structural Correspondence Learning. In *EMNLP*, 2006.

Blitzer, J., Crammer, K., Kulesza, A., Pereira, F., and Wortman, J. Learning Bounds for Domain Adaptation. In *NIPS*, 2007a.

Blitzer, J., Dredze, M., and Pereira, F. Biographies, Bollywood, Boom-boxes and Blenders: Domain Adaptation for Sentiment Classification. In *ACL*, 2007b.

Cesa-Bianchi, Nicolò, Gentile, Claudio, and Zaniboni, Luca. Worst-Case Analysis of Selective Sampling for Linear Classification. *JMLR*, 7, 2006.

Chan, Y. S. and Ng, H. T. Domain adaptation with active learning for word sense disambiguation. In *ACL*, 2007.

Cohn, David, Atlas, Les, and Ladner, Richard. Improving Generalization with Active Learning. *Machine Learning*, 15(2), 1994.

Daumé, III, Hal and Marcu, Daniel. Domain adaptation for statistical classifiers. *Journal of Artificial Intelligence Research*, 26(1), 2006.

Daumé III, H. Frustratingly Easy Domain Adaptation. In *ACL*, 2007.

Finkel, Jenny Rose and Manning, Christopher D. Hierarchical Bayesian domain adaptation. In *NAACL*, pp. 602–610, Morristown, NJ, USA, 2009.

Settles, B. Active Learning Literature Survey. In *Computer Sciences Technical Report 1648*, University of Wisconsin-Madison, 2009.

Shi, Xiaoxiao, Fan, Wei, and Ren, Jiangtao. Actively Transfer Domain Knowledge. In *ECML/PKDD (2)*, 2008.

Sugiyama, M., Nakajima, S., Kashima, H., von Bünau, P., and Kawanabe, M. Direct Importance Estimation with Model Selection and Its Application to Covariate Shift Adaptation. In *NIPS*, 2007.

Parallel Active Learning: Eliminating Wait Time with Minimal Staleness

Robbie Haertel, Paul Felt, Eric Ringger, Kevin Seppi
Department of Computer Science
Brigham Young University
Provo, Utah 84602, USA
rah67@cs.byu.edu, pablofelt@gmail.com,
ringger@cs.byu.edu, kseppi@cs.byu.edu
http://nlp.cs.byu.edu/

Abstract

A practical concern for Active Learning (AL) is the amount of time human experts must wait for the next instance to label. We propose a method for eliminating this wait time independent of specific learning and scoring algorithms by making scores always available for all instances, using old (stale) scores when necessary. The time during which the expert is annotating is used to train models and score instances–in parallel–to maximize the recency of the scores. Our method can be seen as a parameterless, dynamic batch AL algorithm. We analyze the amount of staleness introduced by various AL schemes and then examine the effect of the staleness on performance on a part-of-speech tagging task on the Wall Street Journal. Empirically, the parallel AL algorithm effectively has a batch size of one and a large candidate set size but eliminates the time an annotator would have to wait for a similarly parameterized batch scheme to select instances. The exact performance of our method on other tasks will depend on the relative ratios of time spent annotating, training, and scoring, but in general we expect our parameterless method to perform favorably compared to batch when accounting for wait time.

1 Introduction

Recent emphasis has been placed on evaluating the effectiveness of active learning (AL) based on realistic cost estimates (Haertel et al., 2008; Settles et al., 2008; Arora et al., 2009). However, to our knowledge, no previous work has included in the cost measure the amount of time that an expert annotator must wait for the active learner to provide instances. In fact, according to the standard approach to cost measurement, there is no reason not to use the theoretically optimal (w.r.t. a model, training procedure, and utility function) (but intractable) approach (see Haertel et al., 2008).

In order to more fairly compare complex and time-consuming (but presumably superior) selection algorithms with simpler (but presumably inferior) algorithms, we describe "best-case" (minimum, from the standpoint of the payer) and "worst-case" (maximum) cost scenarios for each algorithm. In the best-case cost scenario, annotators are paid only for the time they spend actively annotating. The worst-case cost scenario additionally assumes that annotators are always on-the-clock, either annotating or waiting for the AL framework to provide them with instances. In reality, human annotators work on a schedule and are not always annotating or waiting, but in general they expect to be paid for the time they spend waiting for the next instance. In some cases, the annotator is not paid directly for waiting, but there are always opportunity costs associated with time-consuming algorithms, such as time to complete a project. In reality, the true cost usually lies between the two extremes.

However, simply analyzing only the best-case cost, as is the current practice, can be misleading, as illustrated in Figure 1. When excluding waiting time for a particular selection algorithm[1] ("AL Annotation Cost Only"), the performance is much bet-

[1] We use the ROI-based scoring algorithm (Haertel et al., 2008) and the zero-staleness technique, both described below.

Proceedings of the NAACL HLT 2010 Workshop on Active Learning for Natural Language Processing, pages 33–41,
Los Angeles, California, June 2010.

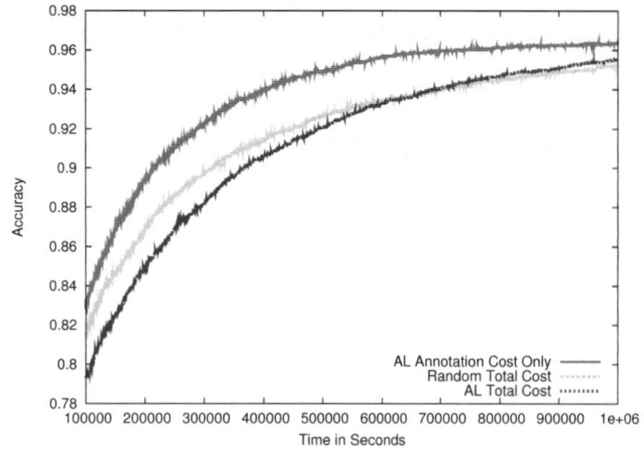

Figure 1: Accuracy as a function of cost (time). Side-by-side comparison of best-case and worst-case cost measurement scenarios reveals that not accounting for the time required by AL to select instances affects the evaluation of an AL algorithm.

ter than the cost of random selection ("Random Total Cost"), but once waiting time is accounted for ("AL Total cost"), the AL approach can be worse than random. Given only the best-case cost, this algorithm would appear to be very desirable. Yet, practitioners would be much less inclined to adopt this algorithm knowing that the worst-case cost is potentially no better than random. In a sense, waiting time serves as a natural penalty for expensive selection algorithms. Therefore, conclusions about the usefulness of AL selection algorithms should take both best-case and worst-case costs into consideration.

Although it is current practice to measure only best-case costs, Tomanek et al. (2007) mention as a desideratum for practical AL algorithms the need for what they call fast selection time cycles, i.e., algorithms that minimize the amount of time annotators wait for instances. They address this by employing the batch selection technique of Engleson and Dagan (1996). In fact, most AL practitioners and researchers implicitly acknowledge the importance of wait time by employing batch selection.

However, batch selection is not a perfect solution. First, using the tradtional implementation, a "good" batch size must be specified beforehand. In research, it is easy to try multiple batch sizes, but in practice where there is only one chance with live annotators, specifying a batch size is a much more difficult problem; ideally, the batch size would be set during the process of AL. Second, traditional methods use the same batch size throughout the entire learning process. However, in the beginning stages of AL, models have access to very little training data and retraining is often much less costly (in terms of time) than in the latter stages of AL in which models are trained on large amounts of data. Intuitively, small batch sizes are acceptable in the beginning stages, whereas large batch sizes are desirable in the latter stages in order to mitigate the time cost of training. In fact, Haertel et al. (2008) mention the use of an increasing batch size to speed up their simulations, but details are scant and the choice of parameters for their approach is task- and dataset-dependent. Also, the use of batch AL causes instances to be chosen without the benefit of all of the most recently annotated instances, a phenomenon we call *staleness* and formally define in Section 2. Finally, in batch AL, the computer is left idle while the annotator is working and vice-verse.

We present a parallel, parameterless solution that can eliminate wait time irrespective of the scoring alogrithm and training method. Our approach is based on the observation that instances can always be available for annotation if we are willing to serve instances that may have been selected without the benefit of the most recent annotations. By having the computer learner do work while the annotator is busy annotating, we are able to mitigate the effects of using these older annotations.

The rest of this paper will proceed as follows: Section 2 defines staleness and presents a progression of four AL algorithms that strike different balances between staleness and wait time, culminating in our parallelized algorithm. We explain our methodology and experimental parameters in Section 3 and then present experimental results and compare the four AL algorithms in Section 4. Conclusions and future work are presented in Section 5.

2 From Zero Staleness to Zero Wait

We work within a pool- and score-based AL setting in which the active learner selects the next instance from an unlabeled pool of data $\mathcal{U}$. A scoring function σ (aka scorer) assigns instances a score using a model θ trained on the labeled data $\mathcal{A}$; the scores serve to rank the instances. Lastly, we assume that

Input: A seed set of annotated instances $\mathcal{A}$, a set of pairs of unannotated instances and their initial scores $\mathcal{S}$, scoring function σ, the candidate set size N, and the batch size B

Result: $\mathcal{A}$ is updated with the instances chosen by the AL process as annotated by the oracle

1 **while** $\mathcal{S} \neq \emptyset$ **do**
2     $\theta \leftarrow$ `TrainModel`$(\mathcal{A})$
3   stamp $\leftarrow |\mathcal{A}|$
4     $\mathcal{C} \leftarrow$ `ChooseCandidates`$(\mathcal{S}, N)$
5     $\mathcal{K} \leftarrow \{(c[inst], \sigma(c[inst], \theta)) \mid c \in \mathcal{C}\}$
6     $\mathcal{S} \leftarrow S - C \cup K$
7     $\mathcal{T} \leftarrow$ pairs from $\mathcal{K}$ with $c[score]$ in the top B scores
8   **for** $t \in T$ **do**
9         $\mathcal{S} \leftarrow \mathcal{S} - t$
10   staleness $\leftarrow |A| -$ stamp ; `// unused`
11         $\mathcal{A} \leftarrow \mathcal{A} \cup$ `Annotate`(t)
12   **end**
13 **end**

Algorithm 1: Pool- and score-based active learner.

an unerring oracle provides the annotations. These concepts are demonstrated in Algorithm 1.

In this section, we explore the trade-off between staleness and wait time. In order to do so, it is beneficial to quantitatively define staleness, which we do in the context of Algorithm 1. After each model θ is trained, a stamp is associated with that θ that indicates the number of annotated instances used to train it (see line 3). The staleness of an item is defined to be the difference between the current number of items in the annotated set and the stamp of the scorer that assigned the instance a score. This concept can be applied to any instance, but it is particularly informative to speak of the staleness of instances at the time they are actually annotated (we will simply refer to this as staleness, disambiguating when necessary; see line 10). Intuitively, an AL scheme that chooses instances having less stale scores will tend to produce a more accurate ranking of instances.

2.1 Zero Staleness

There is a natural trade-off between staleness and the amount of time an annotator must wait for an instance. Consider Algorithm 1 when $B = 1$ and $N = \infty$ (we refer to this parameterization as **zerostale**). In line 8, a single instance is selected for annotation ($|\mathcal{T}| = B = 1$); the staleness of this instance is zero since no other annotations were provided between the time it was scored and the time it was removed. Therefore, this algorithm will never select stale instances and is the only way to guarantee that no selected instances are stale.

However, the zero staleness property comes with a price. Between every instance served to the annotator, a new model must be trained and every instance scored using this model, inducing potentially large waiting periods. Therefore, the following options exist for reducing the wait time:

1. Optimize the learner and scoring function (including possible parallelization)

2. Use a different learner or scoring function

3. Parallelize the scoring process

4. Allow for staleness

The first two options are specific to the learning and scoring algorithms, whereas we are interested in reducing wait time independent of these in the general AL framework. We describe option 3 in section 2.4; however, it is important to note that when training time dominates scoring, the reduction in waiting time will be minimal with this option. This is typically the case in the latter stages of AL when models are trained on larger amounts of data.

We therefore turn our attention to option 4: in this context, there are at least three ways to decrease the wait time: (A) train less often, (B) score fewer items, or (C) allow old scores to be used when newer ones are unavailable. Strategies A and B are the batch selection scheme of Engelson and Dagan (1996); an algorithm that allows for these is presented as Algorithm 1, which we refer to as "traditional" batch, or simply **batch**. We address the traditional batch strategy first and then address strategy C.

2.2 Traditional Batch

In order to train fewer models, Algorithm 1 can provide the annotator with several instances scored using the same scorer (controlled by parameter B); consequently, staleness is introduced. The first item annotated on line 11 has zero staleness, having been scored using a scorer trained on all available annotated instances. However, since a model is not retrained before the next item is sent to the annotator, the next items have staleness $1, 2, \cdots, B-1$. By introducing this staleness, the time the annotator must wait is amortized across all B instances in the batch, reducing the wait time by approximately a factor of B. The exact effect of staleness on the *quality* of instances selected is scorer- and data-dependent.

The parameter N, which we call the candidate set size, specifies the number of instances to score. Typically, candidates are chosen in round-robin fashion or with uniform probability (without replacement) from $\mathcal{U}$. If scoring is expensive (e.g., if it involves parsing, translating, summarizing, or some other time-consuming task), then reducing the candidate set size will reduce the amount of time spent scoring by the same factor. Interestingly, this parameter does not affect staleness; instead, it affects the probability of choosing the same B items to include in the batch when compared to scoring all items. Intuitively, it affects the probability of choosing B "good" items. As N approaches B, this probability approaches uniform random and performance approaches that of random selection.

2.3 Allowing Old Scores

One interesting property of Algorithm 1 is that line 7 guarantees that the only items included in a batch are those that have been scored in line 5. However, if the candidate set size is small (because scoring is expensive), we could compensate by reusing scores from previous iterations when choosing the best items. Specifically, we change line 7 to instead be:

$\mathcal{T} \leftarrow$ pairs from $\mathcal{S}$ with $c[score]$ in the top B scores

We call this **allowold**, and to our knowledge, it is a novel approach. Because selected items may have been scored many "batches" ago, the expected staleness will never be less than in **batch**. However, if scores do not change much from iteration to iteration, then old scores will be good approximations of the actual score and therefore not all items necessarily need to be rescored every iteration. Consequently, we would expect the quality of instances selected to approach that of **zerostale** with less waiting time. It is important to note that, unlike **batch**, the candidate set size does directly affect staleness; smaller N will increase the likelihood of selecting an instance scored with an old model.

2.4 Eliminating Wait Time

There are portions of Algorithm 1 that are trivially parallelizable. For instance, we could easily split the candidate set into equal-sized portions across P processors to be scored (see line 5). Furthermore, it is not necessary to wait for the scorer to finish training before selecting the candidates. And, as previously mentioned, it is possible to use parallelized training and/or scoring algorithms. Clearly, wait time will decrease as the speed and number of processors increase. However, we are interested in parallelization that can guarantee zero wait time independent of the training and scoring algorithms without precluding these other forms of parallelization.

All other major operations of Algorithm 1 have serial dependencies, namely, we cannot score until we have trained the model and chosen the candidates, we cannot select the instances for the batch until the candidate set is scored, and we cannot start annotating until the batch is prepared. These dependencies ultimately lead to waiting.

The key to eliminating this wait time is to ensure that all instances have scores at all times, as in **allowold**. In this way, the instance that currently has the highest score can be served to the annotator without having to wait for any training or scoring. If the scored instances are stored in a priority queue with a constant time *extract-max* operation (e.g., a sorted list), then the wait time will be negligible. Even a heap (e.g., binary or Fibonacci) will often provide negligible overhead. Of course, eliminating wait time comes at the expense of added staleness as explained in the context of **allowold**.

This additional staleness can be reduced by allowing the computer to do work while the oracle is busy annotating. If models can retrain and score most instances in the amount of time it takes the oracle to annotate an item, then there will be little staleness.[2]

Rather than waiting for training to complete before beginning to score instances, the old scorer can be used until a new one is available. This allows us to train models and score instances in parallel. Fast training and scoring procedures result in more instances having up-to-date scores. Hence, the stale-

[2]Since the annotator requests the next instance immediately after annotating the current instance, the next instance is virtually guaranteed to have a staleness factor of at least 1.

ness (and therefore quality) of selected instances depends on the relative time required to train and score models, thereby encouraging efficient training and scoring algorithms. In fact, the other forms of parallelization previously mentioned can be leveraged to reduce staleness rather than attempting to directly reduce wait time.

These principles lead to Algorithm 2, which we call **parallel** (for clarity, we have omitted steps related to concurrency). `AnnotateLoop` represents the tireless oracle who constantly requests instances. The call to `Annotate` is a surrogate for the actual annotation process and most importantly, the time spent in this method is the time required to provide annotations. Once an annotation is obtained, it is placed on a shared buffer $\mathcal{B}$ where it becomes available for training. While the annotator is, in effect, a producer of annotations, `TrainLoop` is the consumer which simply retrains models as annotated instances become available on the buffer. This buffer is analagous to the batch used for training in Algorithm 1. However, the size of the buffer changes dynamically based on the relative amounts of time spent annotating and training. Finally, `ScoreLoop` endlessly scores instances, using new models as soon as they are trained. The set of instances scored with a given model is analagous to the candidate set in Algorithm 1.

Input: A seed set of annotated instances $\mathcal{A}$, a set of pairs of unannotated instances and their initial scores $\mathcal{S}$, and a scoring function σ
Result: $\mathcal{A}$ is updated with the instances chosen by the AL process as annotated by the oracle

```
B ← ∅, θ ← null
Start(AnnotateLoop)
Start(TrainLoop)
Start(ScoreLoop)

procedure AnnotateLoop()
    while S ≠ ∅ do
        t ← c from S having max c[score]
        S ← S − t
        B ← B ∪ Annotate(t)
    end
end

procedure TrainLoop()
    while S ≠ ∅ do
        θ ← TrainModel(A)
        A ← A ∪ B
        B ← ∅
    end
end

procedure ScoreLoop()
    while S ≠ ∅ do
        c ← ChooseCandidate(S)
        S ←
        S − {c} ∪ {(c[inst], σ(c[inst], θ))|c ∈ S}
    end
end
```

Algorithm 2: parallel

3 Experimental Design

Because the performance of the parallel algorithm and the "worst-case" cost analysis depend on wait time, we hold computing resources constant, running all experiments on a cluster of Dell PowerEdge M610 servers equipped with two 2.8 GHz quad-core Intel Nehalem processors and 24 GB of memory.

All experiments were on English part of speech (POS) tagging on the POS-tagged Wall Street Journal text in the Penn Treebank (PTB) version 3 (Marcus et al., 1994). We use sections 2-21 as initially unannotated data and randomly select 100 sentences to seed the models. We employ section 24 as the set on which tag accuracy is computed, but do not count evaluation as part of the wait time. We simulate annotation costs using the cost model from Ringger et al. (2008): $cost(\mathbf{s}) = (3.80 \cdot l + 5.39 \cdot c + 12.57)$, where l is the number of tokens in the sentence, and c is the number of pre-annotated tags that need correction, which can be estimated using the current model. We use the same model for pre-annotation as for scoring.

We employ the return on investment (ROI) AL framework introduced by Haertel et. al (2008). This framework requires that one define both a cost and benefit estimate and selects instances that maximize $\frac{benefit(x)-cost(x)}{cost(x)}$. For simplicity, we estimate cost as the length of a sentence. Our benefit model estimates the utility of each sentence as follows: $benefit(\mathbf{s}) = -\log(\max_{\mathbf{t}} p(\mathbf{t}|\mathbf{s}))$ where $p(\mathbf{t}|\mathbf{s})$ is the probability of a tagging given a sentence. Thus, sentences having low average (in the geometric mean sense) per-tag probability are favored. We use a maximum entropy Markov model to estimate these probabilities, to pre-annotate instances, and to evaluate accuracy.

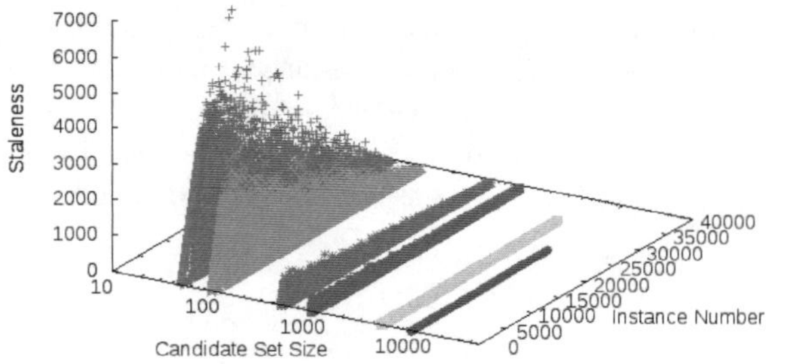

Figure 2: Staleness of the **allowold** algorithm over time for different candidate set sizes

4 Results

Two questions are pertinent regarding staleness: how much staleness does an algorithm introduce? and how detrimental is that staleness? For **zerostale** and **batch**, the first question was answered analytically in a previous section. We proceed by addressing the answer empirically for **allowold** and **parallel** after which we examine the second question.

Figure 2 shows the observed staleness of instances selected for annotation over time and for varying candidate set sizes for **allowold**. As expected, small candidate sets induce more staleness, in this case in very high amounts. Also, for any given candidate set size, staleness decreases over time (after the beginning stages), since the effective candidate set includes an increasingly larger percentage of the data.

Since **parallel** is based on the same allow-old-scores principle, it too could potentially see highly stale instances. However, we found the average per-instance staleness of **parallel** to be very low: **1.10**; it was never greater than **4** in the range of data that we were able to collect. This means that for our task and hardware, the amount of time that the oracle takes to annotate an instance is high enough to allow new models to retrain quickly and score a high percentage of the data before the next instance is requested.

We now examine effect that staleness has on AL performance, starting with **batch**. As we have shown, higher batch sizes guarantee more staleness so we compare the performance of several batch sizes (with a candidate set size of the full data) to **zerostale** and **random**. In order to tease out the effects that the staleness has on performance from the effects that the batches have on wait time (an element of performance), we purposely ignore wait time. The results are shown in Figure 3. Not surprisingly, **zerostale** is slightly superior to the batch methods, and all are superior to random selection. Furthermore, **batch** is not affected much by the amount of staleness introduced by reasonable batch sizes: for $B < 100$ the increase in cost of attaining 95% accuracy compared to **zerostale** is 3% or less.

Recall that **allowold** introduces more staleness than **batch** by maintaining old scores for each instance. Figure 4 shows the effect of different candidate set sizes on this approach while fixing batch size at 1 (wait time is excluded as before). Larger candidate set sizes have less staleness, so not surprisingly performance approaches **zerostale**. Smaller candidate set sizes, having more staleness, perform similarly to random during the early stages when the model is changing more drastically each instance. In these circumstances, scores produced from earlier models are not good approximations to the actual scores so allowing old scores is detrimental. However, once models stabilize and old scores become better approximations, performance begins to approach that of **zerostale**.

Figure 6 compares the performance of **allowold** for varying batch sizes for a fixed candidate set size (5000; results are similiar for other settings). As before, performance suffers primarily in the early stages and for the same reasons. However, a batch excerbates the problem since multiple instances with poor scores are selected simultaneously. Nevertheless, the performance appears to mostly recover once the scorers become more accurate. We note that batch sizes of 5 and 10 increase the cost of acheiving 95% accuracy by 3% and 10%, respectively, compared to **zerostale**. The implications for **parallel** are that stalness may not be detrimental, especially if batch sizes are small and candidate set sizes are large in the beginning stages of AL.

Figure 5 compares the effect of staleness on all four algorithms when excluding wait time ($B = 20$, $N = 5000$ for the batch algorithms). After achieving around 85% accuracy, **batch** and **parallel** are virtually indistinguishable from **zerostale**, implying that the staleness in these algorithms is mostly ignorable. Interestingly, **allowold** costs around 5% more than **zerostale** to acheive an accuracy of 95%. We attribute this to increased levels of staleness which **parallel** combats by avoiding idle time.

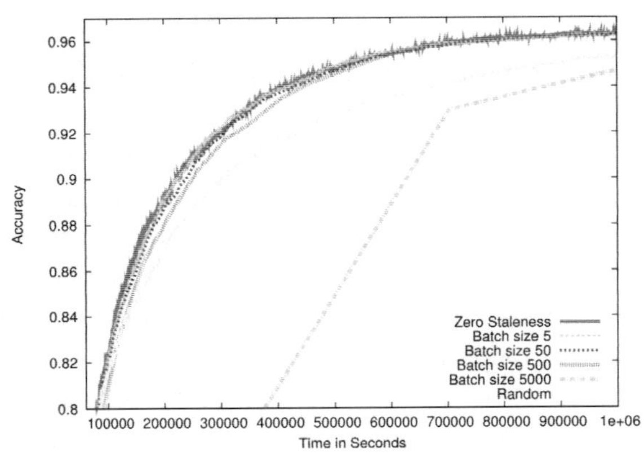

Figure 3: Effect of staleness due to batch size for **batch**, $N = \infty$

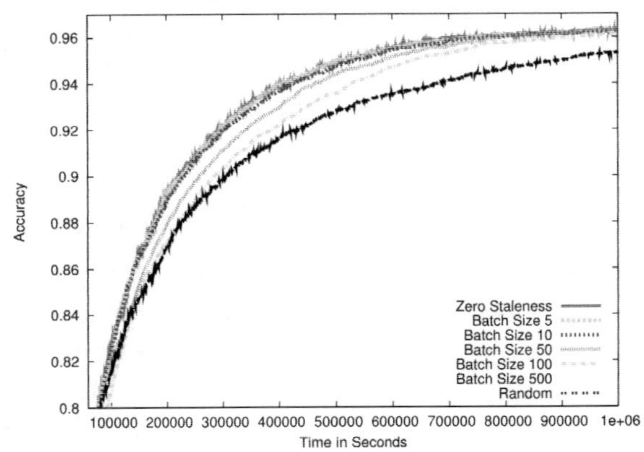

Figure 6: Effect of staleness due to batch size for **allowold**, $N = 5000$

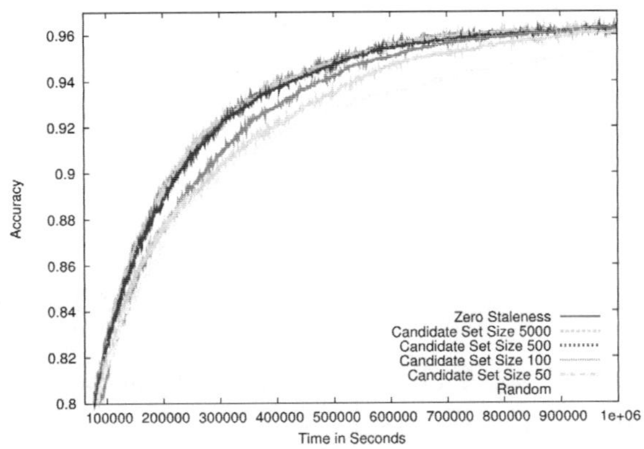

Figure 4: Effect of staleness due to candidate set size for **allowold**, $B = 1$

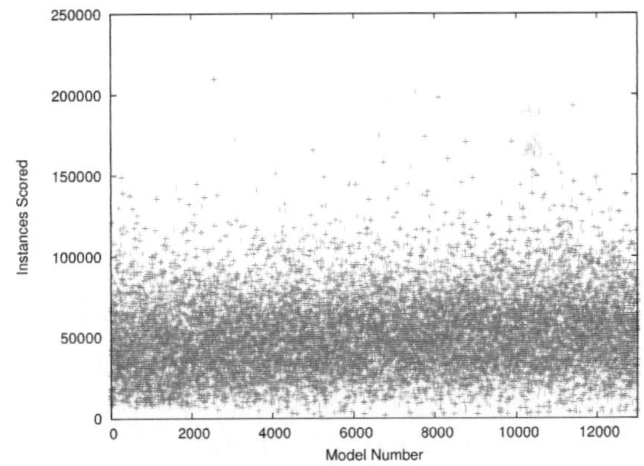

Figure 7: Effective candidate set size of **parallel** over time

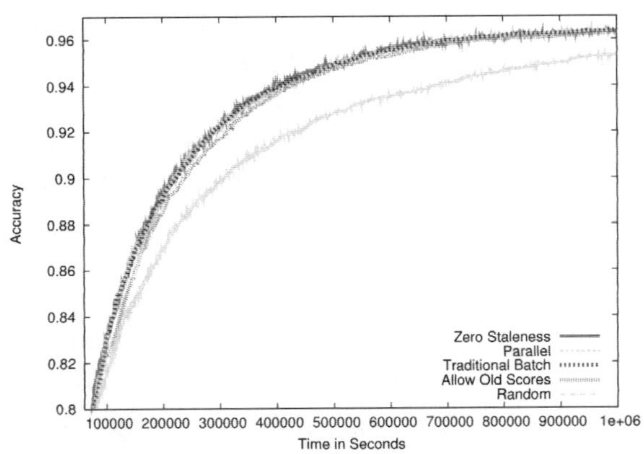

Figure 5: Comparison of algorithms (not including wait time)

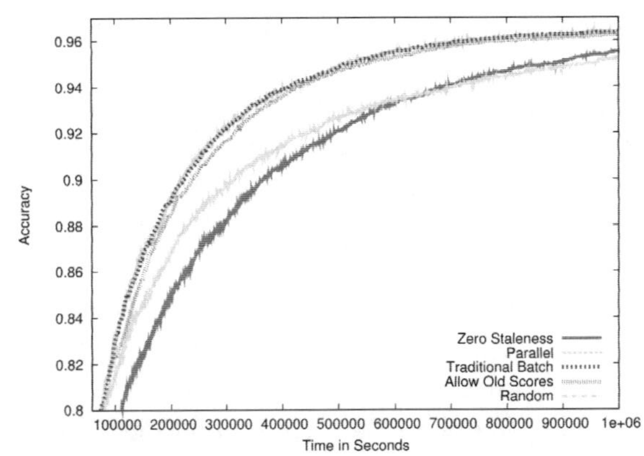

Figure 8: Comparison of algorithms (including wait time)

Since the amount of data **parallel** uses to train models and score instances depends on the amount of time instances take to annotate, the "effective" candidate set sizes and batch sizes over time is of interest. We found that the models were always trained after receiving exactly one instance, within the data we were able to collect. Figure 7 shows the number of instances scored by each successive scorer, which appears to be very large on average: over 75% of the time the scorer was able to score the entire dataset. For this task, the human annotation time is much greater than the amount of time it takes to train new models (at least, for the first 13,000 instances). The net effect is that under these conditions, **parallel** is parameterized similar to **batch** with $B = 1$ and N very high, i.e., approaching **zerostale**, and therefore has very low staleness, yet does so without incurring the waiting cost.

Finally, we compare the performance of the four algorithms using the same settings as before, but include wait time as part of the cost. The results are in Figure 8. Importantly, **parallel** readily outperforms **zerostale**, costing 40% less to reach 95% accuracy. **parallel** also appears to have a slight edge over **batch**, reducing the cost to acheive 95% accuracy by a modest 2%; however, had the simulation continued, we we may have seen greater gains given the increasing training time that occurs later on. It is important to recognize in this comparison that the purpose of **parallel** is not necessarily to significantly outperform a well-tuned batch algorithm. Instead, we aim to eliminate wait time without requiring parameters, while hopefully maintaining performance. These results suggest that our approach successfully meets these criteria.

Taken as a whole, our results appear to indicate that the net effect of staleness is to make selection more random. Models trained on little data tend to produce scores that are not reflective of the actual utility of instances and essentially produce a random ranking of instances. As more data is collected, scores become more accurate and performance begins to improve relative to random selection. However, stale scores are by definition produced using models trained with less data than is currently available, hence more staleness leads to more random-like behavior. This explains why batch selection tends to perform well in practice for "reasonable" batch sizes: the amount of staleness introduced by batch ($\frac{B-1}{2}$ on average for a batch of size B) introduces relatively little randomness, yet cuts the wait time by approximately a factor of B.

This also has implications for our **parallel** method of AL. If a given learning algorithm and scoring function outperform random selection when using **zerostale** and excluding wait time, then any added staleness should cause performance to more closely resemble random selection. However, once waiting time is accounted for, performance could actually degrade below that of random. In **parallel**, more expensive training and scoring algorithms are likely to introduce larger amounts of staleness, and would cause performance to approach random selection. However, **parallel** has no wait time, and hence our approach should always perform at least as well as random in these circumstances. In contrast, poor choices of parameters in **batch** could perform worse than random selection.

5 Conclusions and Future Work

Minimizing the amount of time an annotator must wait for the active learner to provide instances is an important concern for practical AL. We presented a method that can eliminate wait time by allowing instances to be selected on the basis of the most recently assigned score. We reduce the amount of staleness this introduces by allowing training and scoring to occur in parallel while the annotator is busy annotating. We found that on PTB data using a MEMM and a ROI-based scorer that our parameterless method performed slightly better than a hand-tuned traditional batch algorithm, without requiring any parameters. Our approach's parallel nature, elimination of wait time, ability to dynamically adapt the batch size, lack of parameters, and avoidance of worse-than-random behavior, make it an attractive alternative to **batch** for practical AL.

Since the performance of our approach depends on the relative time spent annotating, training, and scoring, we wish to apply our technique in future work to more complex problems and models that have differing ratios of time spent in these areas. Future work could also draw on the *continual computation* framework (Horvitz, 2001) to utilize idle time in other ways, e.g., to predict annotators' responses.

References

S. Arora, E. Nyberg, and C. P. Rosé. 2009. Estimating annotation cost for active learning in a multi-annotator environment. In *Proceedings of the NAACL HLT 2009 Workshop on Active Learning for Natural Language Processing*, pages 18–26.

S. P. Engelson and I. Dagan. 1996. Minimizing manual annotation cost in supervised training from corpora. In *Proceedings of the 34th annual meeting on Association for Computational Linguistics*, pages 319–326.

R. A. Haertel, K. D. Seppi, E. K. Ringger, and J. L. Carroll. 2008. Return on investment for active learning. In *NIPS Workshop on Cost Sensitive Learning*.

E. Horvitz. 2001. Principles and applications of continual computation. *Artificial Intelligence Journal*, 126:159–96.

M. P. Marcus, B. Santorini, and M. A. Marcinkiewicz. 1994. Building a large annotated corpus of english: The penn treebank. *Computational Linguistics*, 19:313–330.

E. Ringger, M. Carmen, R. Haertel, K. Seppi, D. Londsale, P. McClanahan, J. Carroll, and N. Ellison. 2008. Assessing the costs of machine-assisted corpus annotation through a user study. In *Proc. of LREC*.

B. Settles, M. Craven, and L. Friedland. 2008. Active learning with real annotation costs. In *Proceedings of the NIPS Workshop on Cost-Sensitive Learning*, pages 1069–1078.

K. Tomanek, J. Wermter, and U. Hahn. 2007. An approach to text corpus construction which cuts annotation costs and maintains reusability of annotated data. *Proc. of EMNLP-CoNLL*, pages 486–495.

Author Index

Association for Computational Linguistics
209 N. Eighth Street
Stroudsburg, Pennsylvania 18360

CURRAN ASSOCIATES INC
proceedings.com